HESED

LOVE IN THE TRUE MEANING OF THE WORD

Apostle Prophetess Rochelle Graham

HESED
LOVE IN THE TRUE MEANING OF THE WORD
Apostle Prophetess Rochelle Graham
Published by One Faith Publishing
Richmond, VA, Port Huron, MI
onefaithpublishings@gmail.com

This book or parts thereof may not be reproduced in any form, stored in a retrieval system, or transmitted in any forms by any means - electronic, mechanical, photocopy, recording, or otherwise-written without written permission of the publisher and/or author, Apostle Prophetess Rochelle Graham, except as provided by United States of America copyright law.

Scriptures marked NLT are taken from the HOLY BIBLE, NEW LIVING TRANSLATION (NLT): Scriptures taken from the HOLY BIBLE, NEW LIVING TRANSLATION, Copyright© 1996, 2004, 2007 by Tyndale House Foundation. Used by permission of Tyndale House Publishers, Inc., Carol Stream, Illinois 60188. All rights reserved. Used by permission.

Scriptures marked KJV are taken from the KING JAMES VERSION (KJV): KING JAMES VERSION, public domain.

Scriptures marked NIV are taken from the NEW INTERNATIONAL VERSION (NIV): Scripture taken from THE HOLY BIBLE, NEW INTERNATIONAL VERSION ®. Copyright© 1973, 1978, 1984, 2011 by Biblica, Inc.™. Used by permission of Zondervan

Scriptures marked ESV are taken from THE HOLY BIBLE, ENGLISH STANDARD VERSION (ESV): Scriptures taken from THE HOLY BIBLE, ENGLISH STANDARD VERSION ® Copyright© 2001 by Crossway, a publishing ministry of Good News Publishers. Used by permission.

Copyright © 2025 by Apostle Prophetess Rochelle Graham
All rights reserved.

Love... *A pure and timeless word that moves from place to place, from region to region, flowing from an Almighty God to His chosen people.*

Apostle Dr. Prophetess Rochelle Graham presents *Hesed: Love In The True Meaning of The Word* as a powerful foundation of truth, reshaping and redefining what love truly means. With divine insight, she unveils the limitations of past definitions and brings forth a revelation of love that speaks directly to this generation.

In a time when the true essence of love has been clouded and misunderstood, Apostle Dr. Prophetess Rochelle Graham restores clarity and depth, revealing love in its purest, God-given form. *Hesed: Love In The True Meaning of The Word* is a timely and transformative message, perfectly fitting for the world we live in today.

Hesed is the authentic and complete expression of God's love. Unlike anything we could ever know, acknowledge, or experience, the love of God stands incomparable and eternal.

Throughout history, God's love has been described in many ways and through countless terms. Yet, in its purest form, *Hesed* reveals why God continues to love us—through our failures, through our struggles, and even in the moments when we fall short spiritually. This divine pattern of *Hesed* is God's blueprint, showing His people how to embody, demonstrate, and reflect His love in the earth.

This book invites you on a journey beyond the surface of what love once appeared to be, into a higher revelation—where you will discover how God expects you to live, love, and represent Him as love itself in every sphere of your life.

DEDICATION

This book is dedicated to those who are in search of love...

Those who have loved and lost.

Those who have had negative experiences with the "love tag" attached.

Most assuredly, let's not forget those who have never had the opportunity to be exposed to "true love".

FOREWORD

HESED: Love in the true meaning of the word. Every so often, a book comes along that doesn't just inform you — it transforms the way you think about something you thought you always knew.

LOVE…a word that is so broad in its meaning, essence, power, and ability. Could there be even more to this four-letter word?

Yes, there is more!

In Hesed: Love in the true meaning of the word, Apostle Rochelle Graham weaves a fabric of love that is the foundational cloth behind every form of love we have ever experienced or hoped to experience. It's HESED!

With decades of experience in ministry, Apostle Graham has the spiritual depth of revelation to take timeless truths and mysteries within the Word of God and make them both relatable and inspiring." She does this with an authority that commands global atmospheres, sets governmental order, and brings the hardened heart to tears, all within the connecting theme of the Hesed Love of God.

I first met Apostle Graham four years ago when I visited her church through a sister in Christ. I was fascinated when I heard about her incredible prophetic and apostolic mantle. There is a very tangible presence of the Lord that surrounds her. We had a powerful time of worship and encounter with God during that service.

But what made the most lasting impression on me was the immediate feeling of love and humility she showed to me; someone she had just met for the first time. I could see it…I could feel it — it was different. What was "it"? I didn't have a word for it. I left feeling empowered and inspired to learn more from her. God was building a connection through Hesed Love that continues to shape my life even now.

In the pages of this book, you'll discover how Hesed guides us in everything we do for God. You will break free from self-limiting beliefs you have about how completely God loves you and how we are to embrace others in the same type of love as we complete the assignments God has given to us.

This book is for you now. The time has come for you to hear God call us up to a higher realm of love. In an age when distractions pull us in every direction, this book is a call to refocus on how to embody the loyalty that is Hesed love and how our faith, anointing, and very life will depend on our understanding of it. We need this book now more than ever.

I watched for years as Apostle Graham gave her time, gifts, and yes, money to love on and feed the people of God. She would tell me, "I can't charge the people when they are coming to experience God. If God is in this, He will provide for it." It was part of the Hesed love that did not make sense to my analytical mind.

As a pastor of a ministry that empowers women to walk boldly within their God-given purpose, I have developed some expertise in creating events and training as part of their preparation. Most of these events have an associated cost. I trusted that those with financial need who wanted to participate would not be turned away, and God always made sure they were sponsored.

But there was a deeper trust I needed to develop. Could I trust God to supply the thousands that were needed without charging the participants anything? I could not understand that! When I applied just one principle from Chapter 8, I saw a breakthrough in my leadership that had eluded me for years.

Chapter 8 tells us that "Hesed Love will always require adjustments and updates. I needed to update my trust in God's loyalty to me, the ministry, and the women He entrusted to me. I experienced God's provision in an incredible way, as He provided all the necessary funds so that none of the participants had to pay anything.

I encourage you to explore the principles of Hesed presented in each chapter. This is more than a book — it's a guide, a challenge, and a companion for your current and next chapter of growth. Turn the page and start the life-long journey of Hesed.

— Debra Byas

Author of *The Strong One: Godly Wisdom for the Person Behind the Purpose.*

Pastor of Glory to Glory Women's Ministries

Wilmington, NC

Introduction

There Are Many Definitions of Love… Love can overtake the mind and confuse people with misunderstanding, as well as misplacement when encountering relationships on its many tiers. Some might go as far as to say that love is defined as my eyes and heart, but that only leads to utter confusion and displacement of God's true definition of love.

How can we live without love when we were created to love and be loved?

The truth about "love" will be unveiled within the pages of this book. An undeniable truth that will cause a spiritual liberation and a personal elevation. The true concept of love is to be conveyed and conducted in the lives of every living being.

There have been many challenges in people's lives because of "*pseudo*" a love that caused the derailment of purpose, emotional and mental setbacks. Nevertheless, this book will bring an awakening into the light of God's love.

When we say, "We love," we must consider how God loves, and the depth of His love and all it consists of. The love of God is an all-encompassing and substantive love that leaves nothing out and nothing to chance.

You're about to take a journey into love – God's Love – Hesed

Table of Contents

Dedication v

Foreword vi

Introduction ix

Chapter 1: The Love Factor 1

Chapter 2: How Worthy Is Your Love? 9

Chapter 3: Love Goes the Distance 14

Chapter 4: The Love of God Completes and Enhances ... 20

Chapter 5: Love Breaks Barriers 27

Chapter 6: What is Love? 33

Chapter 7: Let's Talk About Love 39

Chapter 8: Hesed Love is Loyalty 42

Chapter 9: Hesed 48

Chapter 10: Workers and Worshippers 54

Chapter 11: Giving you the best that I got? 58

Chapter 12: The Love Factor 64

Chapter 13: The Generosity of Love 69

Chapter 14: Love Comes With Integrity 74

Chapter 15: The Formula of Love 80

Chapter 16: The Strength Behind Love 86

Chapter 17: Who is vouching for you? 91

Chapter 18: Love – Your Round- Trip Ticket 97

Chapter 19: The Capacity of Love 101

Chapter 20: Love Led Destiny 105

Chapter 21: What a Wonderful World it would be! 110

Chapter 22: Finish Strong! 116

Chapter 23: Love Intervenes 121

Chapter 24: Even to our Enemies 126

Chapter 25: Divine Kindness 132

Chapter 26: What you won't do – Do for Love 136

Chapter 27: On Demand 141

Chapter 1

THE LOVE FACTOR

What is Love?

- Love by definition is: A strong affection for another. A profoundly tender and passionate affection for another person.
- Love in Hebrew is **Hesed** – This love is steadfast, rock-solid, faithful within itself, and it's the kind of love that endures to eternity. Hesed is a love that is so enduring that it persists beyond any sin or betrayal to mend brokenness and graciously extends forgiveness.

Hesed is the God kind of love that speaks **LOVE IS LOYALTY**

The Love Foundation

Hesed love is not superficial:
- Only existing or occurring at the surface.
- Appearing to be true or real until examined closely.

Most forms of what we often refer to as "love" have the capacity to draw us in because of the initial appearance. This is how the spirit of enticement allures us into acceptance of another, whether it be friendships, alliances, or emotional marital divine connections.

You must always be aware when it comes to conceptualizing love as it enters the gates of your life. Never be naive in your thinking or misled by placing people in areas of your life or heart, especially placing them where they should never be planted.

Whatever you see at the beginning is never far from what you will see as time evolves and progresses. This is why it's of vital importance that you be prayerful and consistently escalated in the area of spiritual discernment. Doing so, you will never be bamboozled by fleeting fancies and negative toxic connections that will cost you wasted time and unnecessary emotional loss.

Beware of the kind of "love" that has the appearance of being real. The one true thing about the *Hesed love* of God is, it becomes more real the closer you examine it.

In order to test the genuine authenticity of the love in your life, you have to peel back the layers that cover it. Don't just take into consideration the words that people say.

Ephesians 3:16-21:

16 "That he would grant you, according to the riches of his glory, to be strengthened with might by his Spirit in the inner man;

17 That Christ may dwell in your hearts by faith; that ye, being rooted and grounded in love,

18 May be able to comprehend with all saints what is the breadth, and length, and depth, and height;

[19] And to know the love of Christ, which passeth knowledge, that ye might be filled with all the fulness of God.

[20] Now unto him that is able to do exceeding abundantly above all that we ask or think, according to the power that worketh in us,

[21] Unto him be glory in the church by Christ Jesus throughout all ages, world without end. Amen."

This scripture emphasizes that we ought to be:

- ♦ Deeply rooted…
- ♦ Securely grounded….
- ♦ In LOVE!

Doing so, we can experience the LOVE of God to the point that we can comprehend the width, length, height, and depth of His love. To experience this Endless Love, it also says that we come to know God's kind of love through practical experience.

You have to practice:

- ♦ Showing the Hesed love.
- ♦ Giving the Hesed love.
- ♦ Becoming the Hesed love.

In vs.19, it assures us that when we are filled up with the fullness of the Hesed love of God, we will experience the richness of God's presence and become flooded with God Himself.

When people see you going through a hard situation, as people often do, they question your reasoning as to how you can endure. Respond to them by saying, "I am flooded with the love of God!"

When in a hard-pressured situation, it's going to take the power of the Hesed Love to get you through to:

- ♦ The next moment.
- ♦ The next hour.

- The next day.
- The next month.
- The next year.

And as powerful as the Hesed Love of God is…

And as deep as the place of the Hesed love of God is…

In order for it to be fully operational in hard situations, it's going to take humility.

To be Humble:
- Having or showing a modest or low estimate of one's importance.
- An action or thought offered with/or affected by a modest estimate of one's own importance.

Some people often resort to a place or position of contention when dealing with matters of the heart. Especially when they have been wronged or there is some degree of hurt involved. Nonetheless, the power of the Love of God says, Hesed - Love is Loyalty and it comes with humility.

Let's make a comparison between **Humility** and its arch-nemesis, **Arrogance.**

Arrogance vs. Humility

♦ Never admits mistakes.	♦ Admits mistakes.
♦ Doesn't listen.	♦ Listens to understand.
♦ Intercepts conversation/conduct.	♦ Allows others to speak.
♦ Always wants to be right.	♦ Has an open mind.

- Doesn't accept differences.
- Pushes through the point.
- Shows immediate frustration.
- Avoids accountability.
- Creates a "fear me" culture.

- Emphasizes differences.
- Allows ideas to come.
- Demonstrates patience.
- Takes ownership.
- Builds a loving culture.

After seeing the comparisons, you should be able to clearly see the love that is being extended to you:

Is *love* coming from a heart marred with malice?

Is *love* coming from a contentious heart?

Is *love* coming from a hateful heart?

Is *love* coming from a conceited "all for me" heart?

If so, then you can deduce that it's not the Hesed-God Kind of Love.

Hesed Love is Loyalty and derives from humility.

Next, let's compare **Humility** with another arch-nemesis, **Pride**.

What is Pride?

- The quality of having an excessively high opinion of oneself or one's importance.
- Pride is a sin (an immoral act) (a transgression against divine law).

- Proverbs 16:18: *Pride goes before destruction, and a haughty spirit before a fall.*
- Pride will cause you to self-destruct.
- Going your own way.
- Doing your own thing.
- Proverbs 13:10: *Where there is strife, there is pride, but wisdom is found in those who take advice.*
- People who operate in pride refuse to back down, thus creating a doorway for strife to enter and a party of confusion to break out.
- Proverbs 18:12: *Before a downfall, the heart is haughty, but humility comes before honor.*
- The people who are apt to operate in humility will find themselves being honored.

Let the comparisons begin…

Pride vs. Humility

Pride

- Focuses on others' failures.
- Self-righteous, overly critical, and fault-finding.
- Look at their life by telescope and others by a microscope.
- Looks down on others who aren't as spiritual or committed as they are.
- Think they know who is truly proud and truly humble.
- Thinks everyone is privileged to have them involved.

Humility

- Realizes their own shortcomings.
- Compassionate and forgiving,
- Looks for the best in others; seeks to win people, not arguments.
- Realizes only God knows a person's motives.
- They leave the judgment of the heart in the hands of God.
- Thinks they don't deserve the opportunities God gave them.

When weighing the balances, where are you found?

_____

When arrogance meets humility…Humility should always triumph

When pride meets humility… Humility should always triumph.

Hesed Love is Loyalty, and it comes with Humility.

Love functions best through a heart that is genuinely humble, and not superficially humble. Yet, in order to fully operate in the Hesed Love of God, we have to empty ourselves and get rid of the Heavy-weight contenders.

- Pride.
- Arrogance.

And then you'll be able to function in authentic Love.

Hesed is…

- Steadfast Love
- Rock-solid Love
- Enduring Love

- Faithful Love
- Gracious Love

Hesed Love is Loyalty, and it comes with the Hebrew word, Anavah, which means Humility.

Prayer - *Yahweh Almighty, this day I submit to you. Remove from me the Stain of Pride and Arrogance. Cause me to love and operate genuinely in the Hesed of Yahweh all the days of my life. Amen*

Chapter 2

How Worthy Is Your Love?

What is Love?

- A stronger affection for another
- A profoundly tender, passionate affection for another person.

What is Hesed love?

- A steadfast, rock-solid faithfulness that endures to eternity

Hesed is the Godkind of love that is so enduring that it persists beyond any sin or betrayal to mend brokenness and graciously extends favor.

To live the love of God is to Covenant Loyalty. In other words, it denotes trustworthiness.

Trustworthy:
- Able to be relied on as honest and truthful.
- Deserving of trust or confidence.
- Reliable, dependable.

Most of the time, when people express love toward one another, they fail to take into consideration the weight and measure of the word love.

In fact, the word love is often used too lightly, without any thought as to whether there is any substance to it.

Hesed, the Love of God comes with being trustworthy.

It says you can…
- Rely on me.
- Depend on me.
- Have confidence in me.
- My love is honest and truthful.

Hesed is a Love that is honest and truthful, it has no hidden agenda or:
- A secret or ulterior motive.
- Secretly trying to achieve something.

The word "ulterior" means intently hidden. Hesed will never mask the truth.

The word "mask" means to conceal from view. Hesed never conceals, it only reveals truth.

Proverbs 6:16 - 19 displays every aspect that goes against being trustworthy.

"There are six things that the Lord hates, seven that are an abomination to Him:
1. *Haughty eyes*
2. *A lying tongue*
3. *Hands that shed innocent blood*
4. *A heart that devises wicked plans*
5. *Feet that make haste to run to evil*

6. *A false witness who breathes out lies*
7. *One who sows discord among brothers."*

When we operate in the Hesed love of God, you will:

- Not have haughty eyes of pride that make us feel as though we are too big to apologize.
- Not have a tongue that makes you embellish and reshape scenarios to make yourself look good.
- Not have hands that are ready to hit others that Yahweh has assigned us to love.
- Not have "feet" that can't wait to carry evil and execute it against others.
- Not allow you to tell blatant lies about God's people, showing there is no fear of God.
- Not be gossipers, slanderers, and defamers. Sowing discord to try to break up God's ordained connections.

This scripture plainly and boldly says that God hates everything that goes against what it means to be worthy of trust or trustworthy. Many people have made the mistake of trusting the wrong people who were obviously unworthy of their trust.

- Saul was untrustworthy - David trusted Saul as his leader and ended up having to run for his life.
- Delilah was untrustworthy - Sampson trusted Delilah, who was only after money and status. Samson ended up losing his anointing, his position as leader, his eyesight, and his strength.
- Ahab was untrustworthy - Jehoshaphat trusted Ahab to go into battle with him, only to be set up to be murdered on the battlefield.

- Judas was untrustworthy - Jesus trusted Judas to walk with him in ministry. He even trusted him with the ministry's money, only to be left with an empty Treasury account and sentenced to death.

Hesed - Love is Loyalty, and it also comes with being trustworthy.

How trustworthy are you?

So many times, we see the signs...

- The sign that every time you confide in that person, you find out that person has broken confidence and told everyone.
- The sign that every time they need you to stop what you're doing to help them, yet they have every excuse in the book not to help you or show up for you.
- The sign that you know the truth about a situation, but they would rather lie about it with no conscience.
- The sign that you've witnessed them plotting to bring petty revenge against others.

People of God, watch for the signs! Train your spirit man to be trustworthy so that you will be able to identify others who are not trustworthy.

The body of Christ needs more trustworthy people. Not just people that we can count on, but people that God can count on! The Father God Yahweh cannot rely on us to be used if we are not trustworthy.

The Love of God, Hesed - is a steadfast love. In other words, it can be trusted.

How trustworthy is your love? _____

Psalm 13:5 - *"But I have trusted in your steadfast love, and my heart will rejoice in your salvation."*

David trusted in God's love. We too can trust in God's Hesed love because it is a bona fide love.

Let's begin to re-live our love lives toward God!

Let's renew our covenant with God!

Let's begin to live and operate in the Hesed!

Love is Loyalty, and it comes with trustworthiness.

Prayer - *Lord, give me your steadfastness so that the Hesed Love of God can operate through me. So, you can find me trustworthy, and you can use me. Amen*

Chapter 3

LOVE GOES THE DISTANCE

What is Love?

- A strong affection for another.
- A profoundly tender, passionate affection for another person.

Love (Hebrew)

- Hesed - steadfast, rock-solid faithfulness that endures to eternity.

Hesed is a love that is so enduring that it persists beyond any sin and betrayal to mend brokenness, and it graciously extends forgiveness.

Hesed says, "Love is Loyalty"
- No matter what you do to me, my love for you remains steadfast.
- No matter what you say to me, my love for you remains steadfast.

- No matter how you treat me, my love for you remains steadfast.

The reason why the Hesed love of God is so enduring is because it is not based on:
- Feelings
- Emotions
- Happenings

Hesed is based on Covenant!

Covenant love says:
- I'm in this for the long run,
- I'm in it to win it.
- I'm going the distance with you because of my love for you.

In other words, Hesed is a long-term love. When you say the words, "I love you," that means you're willing to love me until the terms of our covenant ends. Based on the example of God's love for us, His love never ends!

Isaiah 54:10 – *"Though the mountains be shaken, and the hills be removed, yet my unfailing love for you will not be shaken nor my covenant of peace be removed, says the Lord, who has compassion on you."*

- God's love for you goes the distance.
- God wants the love you emit for him and others to go the distance.
- Not the kind of love that endures to the length of your driveway.
- Hesed is not short-term love.
- Hesed is long-term love!

Psalm 136:26 - *"Give thanks to the God of heaven; this love endures forever."*

- There is no end to who God is "As Love".
- There is no end to how God extends his love.
- There is no deadline for how God determines to love.

No Deal Breakers

In the Hesed love of God, there are no deal breakers.

For as long as you exist, even beyond your earthly existence into your heavenly transformation, and even beyond that, God will love you!

Deuteronomy 7:9 – *"Know therefore that the Lord your God is God; he is the faithful God, keeping his covenant of love to a thousand generations of those who love him and keep his commandments."*

The governing factor behind how the Hesed love operates is "faithfulness". No one can operate in and live out the Hesed love of God unless they know how to be faithful!

- God is faithful; therefore, Hesed emanates from Him.
- God keeps his covenant of love with us because he is faithful.

Here's another scripture that demonstrates the connections between Hesed and faithfulness.

Jeremiah 31:3 - *"The Lord appeared to him from away. I have loved you with an everlasting love; therefore, I have continued my faithfulness to you."*

The Hesed, the love of God is everlasting. It will cause faithfulness to be birthed in you. Hesed - the love of God will provoke you to be faithful! If someone cannot be faithful to God, they cannot be faithful to you! Even the Book of Solomon references the faithful, steadfast love of God – Hesed.

Lamentations 3:22-23 -

²² "It is of the LORD's mercies that we are not consumed, because his compassions fail not."

²³ "They are new every morning: great is thy faithfulness."

The steadfast love of the Lord never ceases. His mercies never come to an end; they are new every morning. Great is your faithfulness. God's love, Hesed, will never cease toward you. Great is His faithfulness toward you.

The All-powerful, Omnipotent and Omniscient God has committed to being faithful to you, and it ought to be a lightly thing for you to be faithful to Yahweh Elohim.

Jesus was the perfect New Testament example of what the Hesed love of God looks like.

Matthew 26:67 - *"Then they spit in his face and struck him with their fists. Others slapped him."*

Do you know that the Savior of the world was physically assaulted and abused by those he came to save? Yet, he continued to love them Hesed.

Hesed says, *"No matter what you do to me, I will love you."*

Matthew 27:31 - *"And after that they had mocked him, they took the robe off from him, and put his own raiment on him, and led him away to crucify him."*

Jesus was literally humiliated, scoffed at, mocked, and even ridiculed just before his crucifixion. He was treated inhumanely by those he came to save. If Jesus endured such treatment, it should make us even more aware of the "Power of Love".

Hesed says, *"No matter how you treat me, I will love you."*

- ♦ Hesed – A Love that is Loyal and it goes the distance with you.
- ♦ Hesed Love is Loyalty, and it comes with faithfulness.

Matthew 27:40 - *"And they said tauntingly, you would destroy the temple and rebuild it in three days. Save yourself from death! If you are the Son of God, come down from the cross."*

Jesus was literally being called a liar, even on the cross. He was accused of professing to be who he was not! He was accused of not doing what he said he would do.

Hesed says, *"No matter what you say to me, I will love you."*

Don't feel bad when people call you a liar. Saying you claimed to have this or that or saying you claimed to be this or that. Instead, give them a dose of that Hesed love that goes the distance.

They called Jesus a failure, saying he didn't do what he said he would do. So, don't give up hope when you're called a failure. Instead, give them a double scoop of the Hesed love. A love that remains faithful in operating and living out the Hesed love of God; it will challenge you:

- ♦ To change.
- ♦ To see people differently.
- ♦ To walk in a godly way.
- ♦ To leave the old nature behind.

When the Hesed Love of God is truly established in you. You will be like Jesus, and nothing will move you; you'll be able to forgive and remain faithful!

Luke 23:34 - *"Jesus said, Father, forgive them, for they know not what they are doing."*

The Word of the Lord gives us a command to love one another. Therefore, let's begin to live the Hesed Love because it goes the distance, and it comes with faithfulness.

Prayer - *Father God, teach me your Hesed, an unfailing and faithful love. Teach me your ways so that I can love beyond boundaries. Father God, teach me your ways so I can go the distance when it comes to walking in love. Amen.*

Chapter 4

The Love of God Completes and Enhances

What is Love?

- A strong affection for another.
- A profoundly tender, passionate affection for another person.

Love (Hebrew)

- Hesed - steadfast, rock-solid faithfulness that endures to eternity.

Hesed is a love that is so enduring that it persists beyond any sin and betrayal to mend brokenness and graciously extends forgiveness.

Hesed says, "Love is Loyalty."

The Hesed Love **is not** the type of Love that:

- Extracts: To remove or take out, especially by effort or force.

The Hesed Love **is** the type of Love that:
- Supplements: Something that completes or enhances something else when added to it.

The Power of the Hesed Love of God - Love is Loyalty will:
- Complete your life.
- Enhance your life.

To be complete is to be made whole; no longer broken. When you are introduced to the Hesed love of God, you experience Love. Pure Love. A Pure Love that operates far above and far beyond the level of the flesh.

When Pure Love comes into your life:
- It heals you.
- It heals you from the pains of the past.
- It heals you from the conditions that hurt.
- It heals you from irreparable issues.
- It heals you from those areas of brokenness.

This is why experiencing the love of God is:
- Life Changing
- Destiny Altering

The Power of the Hesed Love of God - Love is Loyalty

Enhance your life

To enhance: To intensify, to increase or further improve the value or extent of something or someone. Therefore, and simply put, Hesed has the power to:
- Improve the quality of life and existence.
- Improve the placement and positioning of your value.

- Increase the extent to which you are able to maximize your purpose.

The Hesed Love - Heals and Helps

The Hesed love will never come into your life and see areas that need:

- Repair and not repair it.
- Transformation and not transform it,
- Healing and not heal it.
- Care and not care for it.
- Attention and not give attention.

The Hesed Love - Love is Loyalty is the kind of love that looks and searches out the areas in you that need it most, and Hesed Love fits in perfectly.

Attentive: pay close attention; observant.

Hesed is Attentive

When going on a trip and visiting someone's house, they put out the best sheets, towels, dishes, etc. Doing so, they are ensuring that you as the guest are treated well and you have a need for nothing.

The Hesed Love also ensures that you have what you need and is cared for amply beyond what you want:

- The Hesed Love is an attentive love.
- The Hesed Love of God pays close attention to you.
- Not to stalk you.

3 John 1:2 - *"Beloved, I wish above all things that thou mayest prosper and be in health as thy soul prospers."*

That word "wish" in Hebrew is "PEH". A combination of two words, "mouth and speech," means:
- To yearn for.
- To desire.
- To eagerly desire.

To desire says:
- I long for you to have whatever you want.
- I would love more than anything for you.

The Hesed Love of God completes you in this single scripture, 3 John 1:2

This scripture is basically saying, "Beloved, I want you or would love for you to prosper financially, physically, and spiritually."

The Hesed Love of God has the power to love you into position. To the place where you see the need for change and align yourself to change, and after change comes enhancement. In other words, after you have been completely made whole, your life gets better. Everything is getting better in my life!

God wants your life enhanced and improved in every good way possible, but the challenges come down to you.

Do you want enhancement for your own life? God is giving you the opportunity to walk away from bondage and captivity, but are you giving God excuses as to why the situation is what it is? Guess what?! God already knows!

Question is, what are you going to do?

St. John 5:1-8 - *"After this there was a feast of the Jews; and Jesus went up to Jerusalem."*

² Now there is at Jerusalem by the sheep market a pool, which is called in the Hebrew tongue Bethesda, having five porches.

³ In these lay a great multitude of impotent folk, of blind, halt, withered, waiting for the moving of the water.

⁴ For an angel went down at a certain season into the pool, and troubled the water: whosoever then first after the troubling of the water stepped in was made whole of whatsoever disease he had.

⁵ And a certain man was there, which had an infirmity thirty and eight years.

⁶ When Jesus saw him lie, and knew that he had been now a long time in that case, he saith unto him, Wilt thou be made whole?

⁷ The impotent man answered him, Sir, I have no man, when the water is troubled, to put me into the pool: but while I am coming, another steppeth down before me.

⁸ Jesus saith unto him, Rise, take up thy bed, and walk."

Jesus already knew the facts surrounding the man's current state of affairs. The man had been so weighed down, he had become accustomed to never seeing the change, that all he had left were excuses.

Jesus came to enhance that man's life so that he would no longer:

- ♦ Be alme.
- ♦ Be dependent.
- ♦ Be poor.
- ♦ Be broken.
- ♦ Be depressed.
- ♦ Be represented by the system.

Unfortunately, there are many people today who continue to live their lives REPRESSED by the systems.

- The system of the Economy.
- The system of the Government.

God wants us to understand that when we are in the Kingdom of God. We are not to be repressed by systems because we serve a God of the Hesed, who has power over all the systems of the world!

The man at the pool of Bethesda was being repressed by the system of waiting for one angel in a certain season. He was also being repressed by his own mindset. He thought that he could never make it alone because everyone there was looking for the same thing that he was: **Healing.**

But the power of Hesed says, "Get up from where you are, says God, for I am here to enhance. I'm here to improve and make your life a whole lot better."

When the Hesed Love of God shows up, it changes everything in your life for the better.

- Hesed may meet you lonely, but the Hesed Love will lead you to the desires of your heart, healed and ready for love.
- Hesed may meet you sick, but the Hesed love, and the power of God will heal you of the underlying cause that is truly causing the sickness that is coming upon you.
- Hesed may meet you broke, but the Hesed Love will lead you to financial overflow because you've come to love God and practice the principles of giving that lead to prosperity.

Today, people of God, I encourage you to live the Hesed of God. Let the light of your love shine! Let the salt of your love savor!

Prayer *- Lord, heal me everywhere I am hurt by your Hesed Love and prepare me for the love of my life. Lord, lead me the way that I should go and teach me how to live a prosperous life. Lord, today I renounce bitterness, resentment, jealousy, covetousness, and unforgiveness that have caused underlying sickness in my body in Jesus' name!*

Chapter 5

LOVE BREAKS BARRIERS

What is Love?

- A strong affection for another.
- A profoundly tender, passionate affection for another person.

Love (Hebrew)

- Hesed - Steadfast, rock-solid faithfulness that endures to eternity.

Hesed is the kind of love that is complete with endurance that enhances with persistence.

Betrayal: To violate confidence or trust.

- Hesed breaks beyond the barrier of betrayal.

Sin: An immoral act that is considered to be a transgression against divine law.

- Hesed breaks beyond the barrier of sin.
- Hesed is the barrier-breaking kind of love.

Brokenness: Forcibly separated, sundered by divorce, the desertion of a parent or spouse, a broken marriage.

- Hesed breaks beyond the barrier of brokenness.

Unforgiveness: Unwilling or unable to stop feeling anger or resentment toward someone for an offense, flaw, or mistake.

- Hesed breaks the barrier of unforgiveness.

So now let's break it down.

Endurance

Hesed – Love is Loyalty will complete your love with *Endurance.*

Endurance: The power to suffer patiently through an unpleasant or difficult process or situation without giving way.

In other words, the Hesed love of God will stick and stay through hard, wrenching, and difficult circumstances:

- Mean and inflexible on the job
- Stubborn "know-it-all" employees
- Demonically infused marital relational issues.

Endurance says, "There is nothing that I won't go through for you."

Endurance says, "There is nothing that I won't go through with you."

Loyal Love

Hesed is loyal love.

Hesed is the loyal love that first and primarily existed between God and his people.

Hesed is the loyal love that exists between two human beings.

The major terms of the Hesed Love of God says, "Put Up With It."

When you learn the power of Hesed, you become Hesed!

Micah 6:8 – *"He hath shewed thee, O man, what is good; and what doth the LORD require of thee, but to do justly, and to love mercy, and to walk humbly with thy God?"*

God's people are to do justly, to love mercy, and to walk humbly with and before their God.

1. God expects us to do justly:
- In other words, to do the right thing or live righteously.
2. God expects us to love Hesed:
- In other words, to be merciful towards others and extend His Hesed love.

When you "love Hesed," you can live Hesed.

God also has laid out his definition of the Hesed Love.

Exodus 34:6-7 - *6. "And the Lord passed by before him and proclaimed, The Lord, The Lord God, merciful and gracious, long-suffering, and abundant in goodness and truth,*

7. Keeping mercy for thousands, forgiving iniquity and transgression and sin, and that will by no means clear the guilty; visiting the iniquity of the fathers upon the children, and upon the children's children, unto the third and to the fourth generation."

In verses 6–7, God is saying, His love, Hesed transcends boundaries and is abundant in compassion and loving kindness. He is also saying, those who have committed the trespass against you will not avoid being punished.

Those that:

- ♦ Troubled you… God will trouble them.
- ♦ Hurt you… God will deal with them.
- ♦ Abused you… God will handle them.

God is Hesed, and He is also a just God. Yahweh is a God of Love – Hesed.

Mishpat

God is also a God of judgment, Mishpat.

Everyone wants to embrace the love of God and be encompassed by the love of God. Nevertheless, those who trespass will see themselves as recipients of the Mishpat of God. Those who betray your love and intentionally derailed you will not escape the wrath and judgment of God.

The guilty never get away, no matter how greasy they are. Tell them, "You're not slipping out of this one." Their greasy, slick words won't work because God has seen and taken note of all that has been done and said.

Titus 1:16 - *"They profess to know God, but they deny him through their works. They are detestable, disobedient, and unfit for any good work."*

The Word is plainly saying that: If you claim to know God, then the things you do, say, and act out should be aligned with who God is. No, Mr. Jekyll and Mr. Hyde!

Dr. Jekyll was a well-respected legal practitioner by day. But by night, he transformed into an alternate personality with a murderous and unpredictable nature. He was one man with multiple personalities.

Lord, open my eyes to expose the Mr. Hydes in my life and remove them.

2 Peter 2:3 - *"And through covetousness shall they with feigned words make merchandise of you, whose judgment now of a long time lingereth not, and their damnation slumbereth not."*

This scripture confirms that God is against the people who exploit you and take advantage of you, and that he will bring destruction on them.

2 Timothy 3:11 - *"My persecutions and afflictions, which came unto me at Antioch, at Iconium, and Lystra—what persecutions I endured—but out of them all the Lord delivered me."*

Paul the Apostle, after coming into contact with the Hesed love of God, changed his name and life forever. The apostle suffered and was persecuted in various locations while trying to build up the church, and God rescued him. Just like Apostle Paul, you have been trying to build up people, only to find that you have had to suffer because of their:

- Mishandling
- Misjudgment
- Mismanagement
- Misuse and abuse of you.

Now, because of their mis – they're about to miss you! God is going to rescue. Yes, Hesed is that ending love, but not to the point that God will not intervene when he sees you under severe persecution and distress.

Hesed To the Rescue

In order to remain steadfast in the Hesed love of God – Love is Loyalty. You have to learn to listen and take heed to the word of God.

Proverbs 19:27 – *"Cease to hear instruction my son, you will stray from my works of knowledge."*

Hesed – Love is Loyalty and completes your life with endurance, and it says that you will not have to put up with some stuff!

2 Corinthians 4:17 – *"For our light affliction, which is but for a moment, worketh for us a far more exceeding and eternal weight of glory."*

Beyond all comparison, in other words... What you are going through is going to end shortly, and God will rest on you the weight of His glory, His power, and His presence. To which nothing that you've been through can compare.

When the glory of God comes on you, the pains, memories, and scars are no more. You are no longer afflicted because you're now affiliated with God's glory.

Hesed – Love is Loyalty, and it will give you the power to endure. Hallelujah

Chapter 6

WHAT IS LOVE?

What is Love?

- Strong affection for another.
- A profoundly tender, passionate affection for another person.

Love (Heb) Hesed:

A steadfast, rock-solid faithfulness that endures forever into eternity.

Hesed is the kind of love:
- That completes with endurance.
- That enhances with persistence.

Hesed is the love of God that loves genuinely and authentically with no barriers. Hesed is the barrier-breaking kind of love.

Hesed is so powerful that it breaks the barrier of offense through:

- Sin

- Betrayal
- Brokenness
- Unforgiveness

When we exemplify love from one to another, there are some pertinent factors that we must understand.

Love is pure. Therefore, when we love, we ought to love purely.

Pure: without any extraneous or unnecessary elements; free from contamination.

To contaminate: The action or state of being made impure by polluting or poisoning.

Some people are operating in contamination-love mode.

Their love has become:
- Polluted by adding the elements of flesh and self.
- Contaminated by adding poisons of bitterness, resentment, envy, jealousy, and betrayal.

No one can say they purely love, and they have their hearts intermingled with poisonous elements.

Purify My Heart

Today, we are going to be reintroduced to what it means to live in and operate from a place of Purity in Love.

Read 1 Corinthians 13:4–11

1. Love Never Gives Up.

Pure love never allows or gives place to emotion or addictions.
- When love is based on emotions, you will be unstable because emotions are like waves. One minute you're

happy, and the next minute you're sad. One minute, you're up, and the next minute you're down.

Emotions will make you:
- Stop making an effort.
- Give in and walk away.

This is based on the normal function of relationships, but not in alignment with abusive situations.

Dr. Myles Munroe taught us, *"When the purpose is not known, abuse is inevitable."* When people don't understand your purpose in their lives, they will abuse you.

2. Love Cares More For Others Than For Self.

Pure love will cause you to care where you give attention and be considerate to others:
- Health
- Welfare
- Protection

Read Philippians 2:4

Pure Love Cares:
- Does not merely look for your own personal intentions but also for the interests of others.
- Pure love automatically looks out for you and doesn't put personal interests above others.
- When pure love meets pure love, there is a mutual exchange that creates a strong foundation for the Hesed love of God to be built upon.

- People who don't know pure love will be challenged by the Hesed love of God because Hesed comes with accountability and responsibility.

1 Timothy 5:8 – *"But if any provide not for his own, and especially for those of his own house, he hath denied the faith, and is worse than an infidel."*

God expects pure love in our homes. He expects us to care for and take care of our own, especially husbands.

Galatians 6:10 – *"As we have therefore opportunity, let us do good unto all men, especially unto them who are of the household of faith."*

Yes, God expects us to love and care for those we are affiliated with in the house of God.

3. Love doesn't want what it doesn't have.

In other words, pure love is not covetous with the desire for wanting something or someone that is not yours, and it overwhelms you. Covetousness is a dangerous spirit because it can lead to greed. To the point that no matter how much you acquire, it's never enough.

Luke 12:15 – *"And he said unto them, Take heed, and beware of covetousness: for a man's life consisteth not in the abundance of the things which he possesseth."*

- Be in place to live in abundance, but do not allow it to overtake or change you.

Hebrews 13:5 – *"Let your conversation be without covetousness; and be content with such things as ye have: for he hath said, I will never leave thee, nor forsake thee."*

- As long as you know God is with you, you can have the assurance that you will be taken care of, and there is no need to covet what others have been blessed with!

1 Corinthians 5:11 – *"But now I have written unto you not to keep company, if any man that is called a brother be a fornicator, or covetous, or an idolator, or a railer, or a drunkard, or an extortioner; with such an one no not to eat".*

- Warning! Warning! Stay away from those who are equipped to hurt your life by evil influence, and that includes covetous.

4. Love Does Not Strut.

- To strut means to be arrogant and conceited.
- Conceited means to be vain and excessively proud of oneself,
    - to think everything is all about them
    - to think they are always right
    - to think they are the only ones deserving of a compliment.

Read 1 Timothy 6:2–5

- Conceit will make you do a whole lot of things that are contrary to the Word of God.
- Pure love is not conceited but humble.

If people can't get over being conceited, they will never be able to get into what it means to live and operate in the Hesed Love of God – Love is Loyalty.

People who are conceited are loyal only to themselves and to their flesh, and according to Romans 7:18, *"In the flesh dwelleth no good thing."* Pure love is necessary if you're going to live in the Hesed-Love is Loyalty.

Chapter 7

LET'S TALK ABOUT LOVE

What is Love?

From the world's perspective, it carries a number of functions and can be categorized into different segments.

Love is defined as:

- A strong affection for another.
- A profoundly tender, passionate affection for another person.

In life, we experience several different types of love:

- Philia - deep brotherly; friendship love.
- Ludus - playful love flirtatious.
- Agape - unconditional; universal love.
- Storge - familial; family love.
- Mania - obsessive love.
- Eros - passionate love.
- Pragma - enduring love.
- Philautia - self-love; narcissism; egoism.

Out of all the different types of love that exist in and around our daily lives, none of them can stand close to nor carry the weight of the Hesed Love of God. Hesed is the love that emanates from God and is the essence of who God is!

Read St. John 4:7–21 – *⁷ "The way you love and how you love impacts what happens to you on the day of judgement."*

A point drawn from this scripture is that: Love and hate cannot coexist in a person who is truly loving out of the Hesed Love of God (vs 20). You cannot love God and hate your brothers (people). Can you see me? Then love me!

Hesed is the kind of love:

- That completes with confidence.
- Enhances with persistence.

Hesed - steadfast, rock-solid, faithful love that endures forever to eternity.

The power of Hesed—the Love of God breaks through the barriers of:

- Sin
- Betrayal
- Offense
- Brokenness
- Unforgiveness

Today, we are continuing our exemplification of what it means to have "Pure Love".

Pure Love doesn't have any extraneous or unnecessary elements. `

To love purely - is to love out of a pure heart without poisonous elements such as envy, jealousy, anger, bitterness, unforgiveness, resentment, and betrayal.

Purifying my Heart

Today, we continue the reintroduction process to what it means to love and operate from a place of purity In Love.

1 Corinthians 13:4–11

Previously, we read and dealt with the first 4. Now let's continue so that we can remove everything in us that prevents us from loving purely.

Chapter 8

HESED LOVE IS LOYALTY

What is Love?

Love, as we have come to know it, has been defined as:

A profoundly strong, tender, and passionate affection for another person.

But the Hesed Love of God is *love* on a whole new level.

- ♦ Hesed is a love that is steadfast, enduring, rock-solid, faithful, and endures to eternity.
- ♦ Hesed is a love that is loyal - "Full and Final"

Hesed is so enduring that it persists beyond any sin or betrayal:

- ♦ To mend brokenness.
- ♦ To graciously extend forgiveness.

Hesed loves no matter the:

- ♦ Type
- ♦ Kind
- ♦ Level

Over time, Hesed Love will always require an adjustment. In other words, even love requires an update.

Update defined is:
- ♦ To make something more modern or up to date.
- ♦ An updated version of something.

Let us consider the newest Technological Implementation, "The Application" or "The App". An app is a computer program or software application designed to run on a mobile device (A phone/tablet, etc.).

The original plan was for an app to provide productivity assistance and direct access. Having direct access eliminates:
- ♦ Long wait times.
- ♦ Frustration of information.
- ♦ Having to recall access info.

Over time, the companies that create apps continue to develop the app by removing bugs from electronic glitches. There are times when you may try to use one of your apps, and an "Update Required" message pops up as a reminder.

Update Required

Unless you click the update button, there will be no way to bypass the required update.

When it's required, the only way to get access to the app of your choice is to update.

Updating your app gives you:
- ♦ Access to the most recent and latest features.
- ♦ Improves top security, so there is no enemy infusion.

- Allows electronic stability and continued compatibility with your device.

Please understand that updates will always be required because, although there are no noticeable changes, the technology behind the app is ever evolving.

Without an update, your app becomes obsolete.

Obsolete: Out of date

I'm here to lead you by instruction regarding updating the "App of Love"

App of Love

In your life, an update is required. Many people rehearsed the words, "I love you!"

The ways in which they convey that love are often:
- Misconstrued
- Conditional
- Outdated

People update their apps daily, but never consider the
- Application
- Affectionate
- Personal
- Passion

Love requires an update, or in many cases, it will become obsolete. We may have convinced ourselves that we have marked our love in the lives of the people attached to us. When in fact, what we have been doing is far from what Hesed Love is.

This next level says:
- ♦ You may love me, but your app needs an update.
- ♦ When you do the same things over and over again, you come up with the same end result.

When you're relationally attached, you ignore your love, and when you are ready to access the love zone, you will find the button is broken. It won't be able to respond whenever you hit the "Update Button"

Update Button

Things must begin to change because it's time for the body of Christ to take love to another level. The level of love we are looking to become is Hesed.

1 John 4:7-8 - *⁷ "Beloved, let us love one another. But love is from God, and whosoever loves has been born of God, and knows God.*

⁸ Anyone who does not love does not know God, because God is love."

God is Hesed

The love God has toward us is a loyal love!
- ♦ Loyal love is faithful; it won't cheat on you.
- ♦ Loyal love is enduring; it won't give up on you.
- ♦ Loyal love is persistent; it will go the full length of the journey.
- ♦ Loyal love is rock-solid; nothing will be able to shake the foundation of loyal love.
- ♦ Loyal love is steadfast, it's consistent, reliable, and can be counted on!

Many updates are free, but the Pro levels always come with a fee.

Many people don't mind loving you on low levels because they don't want to pay up for the upgrade.

- ♦ The Pro level love comes with a fee; it's not free.
- ♦ You must give of yourself completely and selflessly. That's a heavy price to pay.
- ♦ You must press to be humble and bottle up every ounce of arrogance. That's a high price to pay.
- ♦ You must operate in self-control, discipline, and not fly off the handle when you get upset. That's a premier price to pay.
- ♦ You must look for the best in people and not the worst, you cannot always highlight people's faults. That's a great price to pay.
- ♦ You have to be willing to stick it out when it gets hard and not look back.

With the Hesed Love of God, you have to put up with everything. Even those people who try you the hardest. Yet, God will rescue you when the time comes.

Therefore:

- ♦ Don't go back to the arms of an ex because of familiarity. It's a trap from the enemy.
- ♦ Don't go back to the addiction that once had you bound; it comes with seven greater demons.

Hesed Love is Loyalty

Read 1 Corinthians 13:4-7

4 Love is patient and kind. Love is not jealous or boastful or proud

5 Or rude. It does not demand its own way. It is not irritable, and it keeps no record of being wronged.

6 It does not rejoice about injustice but rejoices whenever the truth wins out.

7 Love never gives up, never loses faith, is always hopeful, and endures through every circumstance.

Most people don't want to give more of themselves because they are all wrapped up in who they want to be and where they're going. The Hesed Love of God demands that we upgrade.

Hesed Love demands that we update our app:
- Affection.
- Personal.
- Fashion.

Loyal love will make you love genuinely. Genuine love will draw people to the light of the pure love flowing in you. Are you updating your app?

Chapter 9

HESED

What is Love?

Love that depicts the heart of God is called Hesed (Hebrew meaning).

Hesed: Love that is Loyalty.

The very fiber of the Hesed Love of God speaks to a love that is:

1. Steadfast: Resolutely or dutifully firm and unwavering.
    - It will not shift or change with or without a moment's notice.
    - A steadfast love is one that speaks to stability.
    - It remains consistent no matter how circumstances change.

In other words, it's the kind of love that doesn't easily change its mind. God expects us to love from a steadfast and stable place in our lives. Therefore, consider this, an unstable person does not have the capacity to love you with steadfastness.

James 1:6-8 – *⁶"Let him ask in faith, with no doubting, For the one who doubts is like a wave of the sea that is driven and tossed by the wind.*

⁷For that person must not suppose that he will receive anything from the Lord,

⁸He is a double-minded man, unstable in all his ways."

To be unstable in one area will lead to being unstable in every aspect of your life.

Hesed requires you to have:
- Stable mind
- Stable heart.
- Stable emotions.
- Stable ways

Matthew 6:24 – *"No one can serve two masters, for either he will hate the one and love the other, or he will be devoted to the one and despise the other. You cannot serve God and money."*

To be steadfast is to be able to make a choice and stick to it. Not to be teeter-tottering toward one or back and forth. This speaks to instability, which eventually leads to disloyalty. You say you love me, but you're running to the arms of another! That's instability - that's not Hesed.

Loyalty is a character trait that is innately a part of God Yahweh. It's built into His love language toward us.

What is your love language toward God saying?

_____

What is your love language toward your spouse saying?

_____

You cannot love genuinely without applying loyalty. The very fiber of the Hesed Love of God speaks to a love that is rock solid.

2. Rock Solid: Unlikely to change, unlikely to fail or collapse.

This implies that when it comes to the Hesed Love of God, failure is not an option. The Hesed Love of God goes to the place where God loves us from an immovable place.

- ♦ Hesed is the love that won't change up on you. You were good when you were giving up the goods. No goodies – and they're gone!
- ♦ You were good when the money was flowing. No money – no honey! That's manipulation and witchcraft.

Another definition of "Rock Solid" is 'Extremely hard/Impenetrable.

When the Hesed Love of God is in operation between God and His people, absolutely nothing can permeate their relationship.

The Hesed Love of God in a marriage, when in full operation ensures that nothing and no one can get between you and your spouse. Most Americans fail in this area because there are too many people involved in the process of marriage.

To change the chemical composition of a putty soft relationship to a rock solid and impenetrable Hesed Love, you must first remove the water element. Which means, you must remove the watery lips of other people's influence in your life and relationship. Instead, go to God for direction, and he will lead you by the way you should go.

The Rock, His work is perfect, for all His ways are justice of faithfulness and without iniquity, just and upright is He. God is referred to as a "Rock" in His scripture to emphasize His position that is immovable over His people.

The fiber of the Hesed Love of God is…

3. Faithfulness: Quality of being faithful. Fidelity, Sexual faithfulness.

Faithful:
- Remaining loyal and steadfast.
- Faithfulness ties loyalty and steadfastness together.
- You can't have one without the other.
- They are interwoven.
- They are intertwined.

The reason why love fails is because the quality of loyalty is low. It has been diverted to the wrong people and in the wrong direction. The second reason why love fails is because the material quality of their faithfulness is cheap.

- What people value, they put their best into.
- What people value, they are going to give the greatest attention to.
- When people value, they make time and take time to nurture and strengthen.

Cheap love:
- Will tear
- Will break
- Will fade
- Will snag

Cheap love will deteriorate faster than a love that has been built and made *with* interwoven quality.

Knock off the knock off love

The knock-off love:

- ♦ Attracts your attention, but its luster quickly fades.
- ♦ The knock-off love will fit but eventually will tear at the seams because it's low quality.

It's so easy to be fooled by the fabric at first glance. But when you get a feel of the fabric, you know if you're dealing with the real or fake. Don't let the fake love fool you. Feel the fabric and ask God to give you a feel of what the people you encounter are made of. You must test the fabric!

The Bible says, *"Try the spirit by the Spirit."* To try the spirit with/by the spirit is to check for the quality of the fabric's fiber. There are some fabrics by looking at a first glance, you will get fooled, but you could never be fooled by the feel.

Hesed is a LOYAL, STABLE, FAITHFUL, STEADFAST LOVE!

This kind of love, once it's experienced, it changes the very dynamics of your life.

Being faithful brings a great reward.

Proverbs 28:20 – *"The faithful mind will abound with blessings, but whoever hastens to be rich will not go unpunished."*

- ♦ Being faithful will cause you to be blessed.
- ♦ Unfaithfulness brings a breach in the love covenant.

God's love position concerning us will never change. No matter what we do or say, He has commanded His love toward us.

2 Timothy 2:13 – *"If we are faithless, He remains faithful, for He cannot deny Himself. For he cannot deny himself."*

To Himself – God is True

Even when we are not true to Him. Come to yourself and use wisdom to live Hesed and stop connecting with cheap fabric situations that will eventually:

- Tear
- Fade
- Rip

And leave you exposed.

Hesed - Love is Loyalty!

Chapter 10

Workers and Worshippers

What is Love?

I want to take a few minutes and share on M&M's. Everyone loves a M&M in their life, but most people end up being one or the other. Martha or Mary, which of the M&Ms are you?

Read St Luke's 10:38-42

Jesus took a journey from Bethany. A place which means "House of affliction". And because the Anointed One, with all his accounting visited that city. He was on an assignment to deliver the people from affliction.

Whenever God sends you on an assignment. It's because He wants to use you to do something specific and to strategically deliver His people.

Which M&M Are You?

Both M&M sisters carried the same character traits of being rebellious. This was welcomed by both. Martha encountered the anointed room with all His Anointing, and nothing changed for her or about her. She continued being bossy and rebellious.

- ♦ She busied herself with all that she thought was more important.
- ♦ She was distracted by the doings of the day that she considered a vital necessity.

The M&M named Martha missed her encounter with the Anointed One because she was:

- ♦ Too busy to see who had come to see about her.

There are many today, just like the M&M named Martha. They are too busy with life to stop what they're doing to sit and hear what God is saying.

How are you going to know the next move of God if God is speaking, but you don't take the time to listen?

Which M&M Are You?

Martha was the M&M that missed it. She missed the opportunity; the same opportunity that the other M&M "Mary" made exemplary use of. The same character trait of rebelliousness was also a part of Mary. What? Yes, she also came into contact with the Anointed One and all His Anointing, yet…

- ♦ She humbled herself.
- ♦ Focused on Jesus alone.
- ♦ She literally affixed herself in the posture of worship toward Him.
- ♦ Mary was unbothered by the happenings in the kitchen.
- ♦ She put her priorities in place. No food, but focus.

When you want more of God, you have to shut the kitchen down. Focus on God alone and fast. Mary fasted at his feet!

There are specific things that God is doing in this season, and it will require you to fast at the feet of the Father. Zion, I need you to hear the sound! Ministry Family, it's time to pull away from the normal day-to-day doings and make God and the things of God a priority.

Everything that has kept you:
- Worried
- Bothered
- Anxious

These things need to be put out of the line of sight. Just learn in this season to sit and worship God more than you're running around doing unnecessary things.

Are you being bossy and telling people what to do?

St Luke's 10:42 – *"But only one thing is necessary, for many has chosen the good part (that which is to her advantage) which shall not be taken from her."*

Jesus, the Anointed One responded to Martha (the bossy rebellious one's complaint). She was doing all the work, while her lazy sister only worshipped.

What kind of M&M Are You?

Jesus said only one thing is necessary:

Make Him a prioritized focus.

Worship at His feet.

And it would be to your advantage.

What kind of M&M Are You?

Are you the kind that will ignore the presence of God and continue with:
- Church as usual?
- Business as usual?
- Work as usual?
- Marriage as usual?

What kind of M&M Are You?

- Will you be the kind that will recognize God's presence?
- Will you be the kind that will drop your bad character traits?
- Will you be the kind that will pull away from the doings and focus?
- Will you be the kind that sit and worship?
- Will you be the kind that will hear Him and not miss the move of God?

Chapter 11

GIVING YOU THE BEST THAT I GOT?

What is Love?

- Hannah- Grace or Favor.
- Peninnah - Coral; hard, stony substance.
- Elkanah - God has acquired.
- Hesed Love declares, *"No matter how poorly you treat me, and no matter what you say in an attempt to shake my spirit, I will still love you."*
- Hesed Love empowers you to rise above carnal reactions. It creates space for others to be who they are, while also making room for God's power, working through Love to prevent destructive confrontations.
- True Love always takes the higher road. It chooses to love beyond the harmful intentions, attitudes, or actions of others.
- When the Love of God speaks, it reminds you that you do not need to respond to everything.

You will see this clearly in Hannah's story: despite being provoked and antagonized, she did not respond with bitterness, nor return evil for evil.

A man with a heart of acquisition by the name of Elkanah, acquired for himself two wives.

The first wife: Hannah was graced with favor as her name implied. She had everything that a woman could ask for. A husband who named her and gave the greater portion of himself and his assets to her.

She had it all – All except fruit. The fruit of her womb had been stopped. She was barren. In keeping with Hebrew tradition, Elkanah took on a second wife to expand his options of extending his family's name and heritage because he wanted children.

His second wife: Peninnah, whose name meant "coral," had children.

She had 10 sons and 2 daughters. By the frame of the meaning of her name, Peninnah was a hard, stony-hearted dart that flaunted her position of motherhood in Hannah's face.

- ♦ Peninnah never failed to make mention of the fact that Hannah was childless.
- ♦ Peninnah provoked Hannah to respond to her insults.
- ♦ Peninnah irritated Hannah by showing off the fruit of her womb every chance she had.
- ♦ Peninnah made it her goal to embarrass and to make mention of her situation among others.

Hannah dealt with this harshness year after year, until Peninnah gave birth to her 12th child. By the number 12, God had brought Peninnah into governmental perfection. In other words, Peninnah had been assigned to the covenant rights of the 12 tribes of Israel. It was at this point that Hannah knew her situation had to change.

My Situation Has to Change!

It was the number 12 that symbolized God's power and authority, the perfect governmental foundation that pushed Hannah to cry out to God.

When you see the place of God's perfection manifesting around you but not in your life, that means it's time to pull a "Hannah" and cry out to God.

Hannah was grateful and thankful to her husband, who favored her and always gave her a double portion. But seeing the 12, it drove her to fall down in the posture of prayer in Shiloh.

- Shiloh: The place of peace and tranquility.

Hannah found herself troubled, stressed, upset, enraged, hurt, disappointed, depressed, haunted, and perplexed in a place where she should have been at peace. Hannah was unafraid as she prayed and shifted to a higher dimension as she made a vow before the Lord. In other words, Hannah put her name on the line. Hannah was saying to God, "All I have to give, I give you me – my word."

- Vow- Solemn promise to do a specific thing.

1 Samuel 1:11 – *"She made a vow saying, O Lord of Hosts, if you will indeed look on the affliction (suffering) of your handmaiden/ handservant and remember and not forget your maid servant, but will give your maid servant a son then I will give him to the Lord all the days of his life; a razor shall never touch his head."*

Hannah raised the bar in making her vow before God; she was speaking from her heart, "LORD, I'M GIVING YOU THE BEST I'VE GOT!"

Hannah raised the bar, updated her app, and broke the womb of barrenness. When she put her name and vow on the altar, she didn't just put herself as the vow (because to present our bodies is our reasonable service. That's what we're supposed to do.) She vowed to sacrifice the gift of the son God would give her.

Why did Hannah ask for a son?

Luke 2:23 – *"As it is written in the law of the Lord, every first-born male is to be consecrated to the Lord."*

Hannah laid all she had in her vow on the line; she was making one last final appeal. Up to that point, her husband went to the temple to make the sacrifice for his family. But Hannah knew that for this request, she had to make some personal moves. Hannah was saying as she prayed and vowed, "Lord, 'I'm giving you the best I got!"

People, how bad do you want it?

When you want something from God that falls into the category, "I want it real bad!" then it will require that you come to that place where you put your prayer, your vow, and your name on the line and cry out like Hannah. Say, "Lord, I'm giving you the best that I've got!"

In the midst of Hannah pressing for her breakthrough, she came under a misconstrued evaluation. Eli the priest, assumed that Hannah was drunk because of how she was praying, yet he heard nothing.

You have to come to that place to vow and pray and put it all on the line to get God to move for you.

- ♦ People won't understand the move.
- ♦ People won't connect to your vision.

Why? This next level is between you and God! - No third parties!

Hannah had to respectfully inform Eli the priest, that what you see doesn't emanate from drunkenness, but from desperation.

- I'm not drunk, I'm decreeing,
- I'm not drunk, I'm declaring. The release of what I want from God.

When Eli the priest understood, he came into agreement with Hannah.

1 Samuel 1:17 – *"Then Eli answered and said, go in peace and may the God of Israel grant your petition that you have asked of him."*

Don't judge another person's situation until you fully understand what they're dealing with:

- Behind closed doors.
- Beneath the layers.
- Between the sheets.

People are bearing pain that goes deep, so be careful how you approach people because you don't want to hurt or offend someone.

Luke 17:2 – *"It would be better for them to be thrown into the sea with a millstone hung around your neck than to offend one of these little ones."*

1 Samuel 1:17 - *"After her prayer and vow encounter, Hannah was no longer sad."*

1 Samuel 1:18 – *"She went back home and had a romantic evening with her husband, the man who had acquired her heart and Hannah conceived."*

- Hannah remained focused on what she needed, wanted, and deeply desired from God and she received it.

- Had she allowed Peninnah's taunting and constant reminders of her barrenness to distract her. I believe Hannah would not have walked away with the blessing of becoming fruitful.

Hallelujah! Hannah's prayers were answered. Why? She cried out to the Lord. "Lord, I'm giving you the best I've got!" Hannah had a son, a prophet named Samuel, and Hannah kept her vow to God.

When you get tired of complaining, grumbling, being stagnated, being in bondage, being ensnared, being taunted, and being haunted – Level up your Prayer Life!

Level up and make a vow that will get God's attention, "Lord, I'm giving you the best that I've got!" Hallelujah!

Chapter 12

THE LOVE FACTOR

What is Love?

- Love is a strong affection for another person, a profoundly tender or passionate affection for another person.

Love: Heb

- Ahab: an intensely close emotional bond connected to favor.
- Hesed: steadfast, rock-solid faithfulness that endures to eternity.

Hesed is a love that is so enduring that it persists beyond any sin or betrayal to mend the brokenness and graciously extends forgiveness.

Hesed is that love that speaks as: LOVE IS LOYALTY

The Influence of Love

There are many who say they love you, but there is a varying degree of the depth and the quality of love that is being referred. When we love or say we love as believers, we need to understand that as representatives of the Kingdom of God, we must love...

- Which is to love the way God loves.
- God's love for us is also connected to us and His loyalty.

Loyalty: Quality of being loyal.

Loyal: Giving or showing firm and constant support or allegiance to a person, institution, or organization.

- Faithful allegiance (government, country).
- Faithful to a private person the whom faithfulness is due (marriage).
- Faithful to a cause, ideal, custom, institution, or organization. (churchgoer, political party support).

God's love is loyal because God's love is faithful; in other words, you can count on God's love. Up to this point in your life, how have you been loving? Has your love been based on the "Hesed" Love of God, or has it been based on the elation of the moment?

- Hesed says, No matter what, my loyalty toward you will never change.
- Hesed is Love in the long-term.
- Hesed is not the kind of Love that is here today and gone tomorrow.
- Hesed is the kind of Love that will stand with you.
- Hesed is the kind of Love that will support you.
- Hesed is the kind of Love that will pledge its allegiance.

- Hesed is the kind of Love that will be faithful.
- Hesed is the kind of Love that will be firm always.

Hesed is a powerful kind of love because it is not based on:
- Fleshly emotions.
- Current beauty.
- Favorable circumstances.
- Brotherly/sisterly affection.
- Familial connections.

Hesed is based on "Covenant"

Isaiah 54:10 – *"Through the mountains be shaken and the hills be removed, yet my unfailing love (hesed) for you will not be shaken."*

God's love is unshakable and unmovable because it is founded and based on "Covenant".

Covenant: The unwritten agreement of promise under seal between two or more parties to the performance of some action.

The action to be performed here is to love by the "Hesed" Love of God. You should never express your love for any person, institution, or organization unless you are ready to unwaveringly be "loyal" on every level and to every degree.

God does not take his love for us lightly because he is loyal. Therefore, we should not take the love of God lightly, but we should begin to become Hesed.

1 John 4:7-21:

7 "Love comes from God the very essence of God is love.

8 Those people who don't show love do not know God, God is love.

⁹ Love is also an act of giving and sacrifice. God gave up his only son (a part of himself to die as a sacrifice) so that we could live.

¹¹ Since God loves us by the Hesed, we should also love his people by Hesed.

¹² To see God is to display his love through your life and His Hesed will become perfected in you.

Whatever you practice, you perfect

¹³ God's love has the capacity to abide within us because God has given us his spirit. The Holy Spirit (also another part of himself)

God is giving Himself to us but it's up to us to accept Him into our lives.

¹⁵ If we declare that Jesus is the Son of God, we live in union with God and God lives in union with us.

¹⁶ We need to come into the knowledge of the true Love of God; So that we can understand and believe the love God has for us.

¹⁷ God wants his love perfected in us to prepare us for the day of judgment.

¹⁸ There is no fear in love. Perfect love eliminates fear.

- ♦ The fear of the unknown.
- ♦ The fear of death.
- ♦ The fear of the vicissitudes of life.

When the love of God (Hesed) has been perfected in you, you will never operate or fail ever again in your life.

¹⁹ We have been given the capacity to love because God made us His love (Hesed) available to us first.

²⁰ To hate others puts you in the category of a liar.

You can never love God without loving those He created because God's covenant of love covers all mankind." All homo sapiens: All loved by God... Hesed

²¹ God has given his command personally to each of us."

Whoever loves God (and to love God is to be loyal to him) must also love their brother/sister (all people) and love them as God loves. With a love that is loyal, faithful, firm, and unshakable – Hesed.

Chapter 13

THE GENEROSITY OF LOVE

What is Love?

Love is a strong affection for another person, a profoundly tender or passionate affection for another person.

Love: Heb

Ahab: an intensely close emotional bond connected to favor.

Hesed: steadfast, rock-solid faithfulness that endures to eternity.

Hesed is a love that is so enduring that it persists beyond any sin or betrayal to mend the brokenness and graciously extends forgiveness.

Hesed is that love that speaks as:

LOVE IS LOYALTY

Hesed speaks of an indescribable kindness and generosity done by a person who is in a place of power. God exposed His love to his people, the Israelites. Through his generosity, even when the children of Israel forgot God and broke the covenant – God kept covenant with them.

Psalm 89:34 - *"My covenant I will not break nor alter the thing (utterance) that is gone out of my lips."*

God keeps the words of his covenant, and He performs His words. God showed up every time the children of Israel needed Him. Even when they had the wrong approach – because unlike human/people, the deity and sovereignty of God is not fickle or unstable.

God will, is, and will always be:
- Faithful – Remaining loyal and steadfast.
- True – Accurate without variation, real.
- Upright – Strictly honorable and honest.
- Generous – larger or more than is usual or necessary; showing kindness toward others; readiness to give more of something.

The Hebrew word Hesed is not just a feeling – it's an action.

When people think of love, they think of how they FEEL about something or someone, doing so, they can clarify and quantify the level of 'Love' they have.

The Hesed of God has no limitation because it is a generous form of love. The Hesed love of God acts out unvarying love, especially to those who deserve it.

The Hesed love of God goes the extra mile, especially for those who are thankful.

Hesed will be felt and seen, even if at first it is ignored. The Hesed love of God will stand in the gap, place a hedge around you, and pray over others to keep them in a place of peace.

Hesed love serves generosity in many forms:
- ♦ Giving of personal time.
- ♦ Giving of gifts/talents where needed.
- ♦ Giving of personal resources to close the breach.

A Hesed kind of love says that you can count on me to show up, I can be counted on no matter what I'm enduring or going through, or how long I have to go through it.

Hesed is not about arousing fleshly passion or the thrill of romance, but it's about the kind of security that comes with faithfulness and loyalty.

The Hesed of God and His generosity was evident over the children of Israel. God released an unrelinquishing blessing over them.

Numbers 6:22-27 – *"God spoke to Moses, tell Aaron and his sons. This is how you are to bless the people of Israel say to them, "God bless you and keep you. God smile on you and gift you. God look you full in the face and make you prosper. In so doing they will place my name on the people of Israel. I will confirm it by blessing them."*

The generosity of the love of God – Hesed was seen and felt, and that very same level of generosity is extended to you.

Exodus 15:22-27 (read)

The children of Israel needed water, and they were exhausted. The waters were transformed from bitter waters to sweet waters because God loved them and didn't want to see them suffer.

When someone loves you:

1. They will never want to see you suffer.

2. They would never want to be the source of your suffering.

3. They would do everything in their power to eliminate suffering on every level from your life.

The Hesed of God manifested in generosity to eliminate suffering from the midst of the children of Israel. Yet, all the love God had for the children of Israel, their words towards God never reflected any level of reciprocation. God gave Hesed but never received Hesed in return.

Exodus 16:1-31 (read)

The "if only" statements were direct words with the intent to bring hurt to God. The children of Israel were reflecting with regret after leaving bondage and taking God's plan to the Promised Land. When we say, "if only," we're saying to God we don't appreciate what God has done or who God has given us.

A marginal wife saying to her husband, "If only" I had married Obama, at least he would have loved me and put me in a prestigious position". Imagine a husband saying to his wife, "If only" I had married Elaine, I would have been happy in marriage."

Those scenarios are not based on the love of God. The Hesed of God would never break you down what built you up. God extended the Hesed, but it was not appreciated. Time after time, the children of Israel cried out and complained. Still, God showed up in the Hesed Love in generosity because whatever God does, He does with generosity.

The Hebrew word for generosity is 'Berakah'.
- Blessed
- Most blessed
- Gift
- Blessings

The Hesed of God is love, and it shows up with generosity.

Berakah, the love of God – Hesed comes with blessings even when others around you don't:
- ♦ See your love.
- ♦ Acknowledge your love.
- ♦ Return your level of love.
- ♦ Accept your love.

Continue to live in the Hesed of God.

Hesed – Love is loyalty and comes with generosity.

Be generous with your:
- ♦ Kindness
- ♦ Mercy
- ♦ Compassion
- ♦ Time

Whatever we do, we represent our God Yahweh Almighty and the Kingdom of God, and it all comes down to love! Hesed – Love is Loyalty

Chapter 14

Love Comes With Integrity

What is Love?

Love is a strong affection for another person, a profoundly tender or passionate affection for another person.

Love: Heb

Ahab: an intensely close emotional bond connected to favor.

Hesed: steadfast, rock-solid faithfulness that endures to eternity.

Hesed is a love that is so enduring that it persists beyond any sin or betrayal to mend the brokenness and graciously extends forgiveness.

Hesed is a love that is so enduring that it persists beyond any sin or betrayal to mend brokenness and graciously extends favor.

To live the love of God – Hesed is to live covenant loyalty. In order for covenant loyalty to be upheld, the person needs to know and understand how to operate with integrity.

What is integrity?
- ♦ The quality of being honest and having strong moral principles.
- ♦ Moral of brightness.
- ♦ The state of being whole and undivided.
- ♦ Internal consistency or lack of corruption.

God's love toward us comes with generosity, and it also comes with integrity.

Micah 6:8

"He has told you, man what is good and what does the Lord require of you to do justice, and to love mercy/ kindness and to walk humbly with your God."

The Lord's mercy/ kindness verse refers to Hesed - The covenant loyalty of love.

It's interesting to note that in this verse, integrity is named first…
- ♦ To do justice or to do justly speaks of integrity.
- ♦ To remain committed to the faithfulness that Hesed demands, you must be able to live it out with integrity.

We've seen over time and throughout Biblical history that some people have shown some forms of loyalty in their love and commitment to each other. Yet have failed to act with integrity.

1 Samuel 24:10-13

In this narrative, the author is David.

Saul was in hot pursuit of David's life because he was inflamed with jealousy against David's favor with God and man. David, being a man of war and knowing how to move stealthily, had the opportunity to kill Saul and literally wipe out his enemy.

So, it was indisposed, which means he was in one of those rare moments when the king was left unguarded. He was alone, he was vulnerable, and yet David didn't kill him.

David loved Saul as he loved his son, Jonathan. David was consciously stricken in the moment of the opportunity to seize the life of the one trying to take him out. Instead, he took evidence; he cut off a piece of the King's robe as evidence that he was that close to him. Yet he left him alive. For David to kill Saul would be for him to break his love, loyalty, and Hesed covenant with God.

[10] *"I will not lay my hand on my lord because he is the Lord's anointed.*

David did the right thing; he acted with integrity and pleased God. David acknowledged the fact that the anointing of God was still upon Saul, whether he liked it or not. And to hurt God's anointed would be to cross those lines.

[12] *"May the Lord judge between you and me. And may the Lord avenge the wrongs you have done to me, but my hand will not touch you."*

David did the right thing. He stood upright in his integrity, and he refused to break his covenant, love, and loyalty to God.

David told Saul plainly in verse 13.

[13] *"As the old saying goes. From evil does come evil deeds, so my hand will not touch you. I leave you to God."*

Integrity - moral uprightness caused David to do the right thing, whether he wanted to or not.

Micah 6:8 – *"The Lord calls for you to do justly, act with justice, do the right thing with no exceptions."*

It doesn't say do the right thing, act the right way, or treat people right "UNTIL"

- Someone makes you mad.
- Someone betrays you.
- Someone attacks you.
- Someone takes advantage of you.
- Someone defames your character.
- Someone humiliates you.
- Someone steals from you.
- Someone laughs at you or your vision.
- Someone hurts you.
- Someone gets your promotion.
- Someone steals your spouse.
- Someone gets on your last nerve.
- Someone steals your opportunities.

No! There are no exceptions given – you must do the right thing 365 days a year/ 24 hours a day.

Zachariah 7:9 backs this up. *"Thus saith the Lord of Hosts, Render true judgments, show kindness and mercy to one another."*

If you doubted Micah 6:8, there's your backup. God said it, it says what He means, and He means what he says.

Titus 1:8 - *"But be hospitable, a lover of good, self-controlled, upright, holy and disciplined."*

It took self-control, uprightness, and being a lover of doing good to keep David from killing Saul because only the weak give in. It's the strong that don't give in to the whims of the flesh. In those precarious situations, God is expecting to see the Hesed love is loyalty, that comes with integrity.

The words love and mercy in Micah 6:8 refer to Hesed love, and it comes with doing justly or walking with integrity. People say they love God, but they act outside the lines of integrity when it comes to being loyal. "These people aren't loyal!"

People say they love you, but they display levels of distrust toward you by:

- By betraying you every time.
- By belittling you every time.
- By throwing you under the bus every time.

May God remove the people who say they love you but don't have integrity. It's Hesed or Nothing at all!

You may have compromised your entire life, but in this season, you cannot afford to compromise in the area of love. You need the real deal! Hesed or Nothing.

You need the kind of love that will do right by you in integrity, just because it's the right thing to do. Hesed love is loyalty, and it comes with integrity.

- Can I trust your love?
- How deep in integrity is your love?

Psalm 7:8 – *"The Lord judges the people; judge me oh Lord according to my righteousness and according to the integrity that is in me."*

If the roll call for integrity were called right now, would you make the list?

Integrity will make you wait on God. You will wait on God for the right spouse instead of sleeping around with every friend you have - your coworkers and everyone in the church.

Hesed or Nothing!

You will wait on God for the right season to invest/buy instead of jumping up to buy just because everyone else is buying. Integrity will set the matters of your heart in order.

Request from God… Lord, give me integrity that I may do the right thing in every area of my life and every season of my life.

Hesed or Nothing!

Love is loyalty, and it comes with integrity. Hesed Love is Loyalty, and it imprints your love on me.

Chapter 15

THE FORMULA OF LOVE

What is Love?

Love is a strong affection for another person, a profoundly tender or passionate affection for another person.

Love: Heb

Ahab: an intensely close emotional bond connected to favor.

Hesed: steadfast, rock-solid faithfulness that endures to eternity.

Hesed is a love that is so enduring that it persists beyond any sin or betrayal to mend the brokenness and graciously extends forgiveness.

Hesed is the love of God, and it comes with depth – it's deep.

Hesed is the love of God, and it requires action. It requires an actual form of demonstration.

The Hesed of God is a love based on covenant. The covenant and love agreement between God and His people. It is in this Hesed covenant that God shows His:

1. Kindness

2. Loyal love

The most profound thing about the Hesed love of God is that it has absolutely nothing to do with emotions.

Emotions - a natural instinctive state of mind deriving from one's circumstances, mood, or relationship with others.

All of which affects:
- Mood
- Circumstances
- Relationships

Emotions will shift, change, and can be unstable.

Hesed is a loyal love that is stable.

Hesed love is loyalty, and it comes with stability.

In the book of Ruth, we can see what the Hesed love looks like and its stability.

Ruth 1:1-9

"Naomi had lost her husband and had made a decision to return home.

In the midst of that she knew she was now old, but her two daughters-in-law were still young.

She wanted them to have another opportunity to love."

In verse 8, Naomi bestowed upon them the Hesed love of God (kindness).

"May God show you the same kindness you have given me. Not just her but to her my husband and her husband and her son who were now dead.

Both Ruth and Orpah had remained loyal and their love - to their father-in-law until he died and to both their husbands and tell their death."

"And now the police and position of loyalty had been transferred to their mother-in-law, Naomi."

Loyalty within itself is hard to find. Loyalty that is consistent and stable is even harder to find. Hesed Love is loyalty, and it comes with stability. This is the kind of love that says:

- No matter the changes you face – Hesed.
- No matter the challenges you encounter – Hesed.
- No matter the loss you take – Hesed.

Some people will say they love you and not realize that they are truly operating outside the parameters of the Hesed. They say they will love you, but they are ready to leave and desert you when your assets are depleted. That's because their motives behind what they were doing were selfish. They claim to love you, but they only want access to what you have.

They say that they love you, but they refuse to step out of self to make any sacrifices with you in mind. That's because they are so wrapped up in themselves, they think everything is always about them and what they want.

- Hesed will remain the same.
- Hesed brings stability to the table.

Deuteronomy 32:4 - *"The rock! This work is perfect; for all his ways are just; a God of faithfulness and without injustice, righteous and upright is He."*

The very embodiment of God and His character reflects that which is rock solid, and so is His love toward us. Hesed – it's rock solid and it's stable, not shaking, it's firmly fixed and not wishy washy.

It's important to note that when your life is fixed, the people who say they love you with their version of love, one day they love you, the next day they don't. It will make your life unstable, and therefore, you must follow…

Proverbs 4:23 - *"Guard your heart with all diligence, for out of the heart flows the issues of life."*

When you let down the guard of your heart, make sure that you're letting in the Hesed Love of God. Make sure it's not an impostor or an imitator of the Hesed.

Many imitators have:
- The right look.
- The right talk.
- The right walk.

But when it all comes together, there is no:
- No Hesed
- No Covenant Love
- No Stability
- No Rock-Solid Love

With Naomi and Ruth, you can see the reflection of the Hesed when Naomi was looking out for her "still young" daughters-in-law's best interests. Ruth experienced the Hesed love, so she began to live out, reflect, and convey the Hesed onto Naomi.

Ruth 14-19:

"Orpah left, but Ruth stayed.

Ruth stayed because her love was steadfast and rock solid.

What she saw in Naomi taught Ruth how to operate in the Hesed love of God.

Even when Naomi gave her the option to leave and try to push her away, her love remained steadfast.'

Hesed Love is Loyalty, and it comes with stability.

In other words, I'm staying with you for the full length of the journey.

16 And Ruth said, entreat me not to leave thee or to return from following after the: for whither thou goest I will go and where thou lodgest I will lodge; thy people shall be my people and thy God shall be my God.

The Hesed Love of God is a stable love that is totally, completely, and genuinely devoted. Ruth was devoted to Naomi… that means she would never allow anything or anyone to get between her and Naomi.

Let's take a moment to examine the love relationships in our own lives.

- Are you the placard of Hesed like Naomi was to Ruth?_____
- Are you the reflection of what the Hesed love looks like, rock solid and stable?_____
- Are you completely and genuinely committed to the people who sit in the seat of love in your life?_____
- Is there a complete and utmost devotion from you to the people in your life?_____

STOP!

We have to come to a place when we just stop!

S - See the valuable asset you are in God.

T - Take the seat of control from those who are unqualified to drive in your life.

O - Open your heart with the true power of love, the Hesed, and live it out as richly as you know how.

P - Put yourself in a place to be used by God to bring His Hesed love to life.

Stop placing all your love in the hands of people who don't value you and only want to use you. It's time to wise up!! God has a purpose for us to be love, to be the Hesed. Others will see His Hesed and want what they see.

Let this be your takeaway:
- Hesed led Ruth to her Boaz.
- Hesed led Ruth to her destiny.
- Hesed led Ruth to wealth.
- Hesed led Ruth to promotion.

Once you begin to be Hesed:
- Love is Loyalty, and it comes with Integrity.
- Love is Loyalty, and it comes with generosity.
- Love is Loyalty, and it comes with stability.

You will become:
- The change you want to see.
- The solution to the pending problems.

Once you experience the Hesed covenant love of God, everything in your life changes for the good – Hesed.

Chapter 16

THE STRENGTH BEHIND LOVE

What is Love?

Hesed is the love of God.

It is the steadfast, unfailing, rock-solid, covenant love-based love that's enduring and trustworthy.

Hesed expresses God's faithfulness to His people.

Numbers 14:18-19

18 "The Lord is slow to anger, abounding in love and forgiving sin and rebellion. Yet he does not leave the guilty unpunished; he punishes the children for the sin of the parents to the third and fourth generation."

19 "In accordance with your great love, forgive the sin of these people, just as you have pardoned them from the time, they left Egypt until now."

Moses made an appeal to God – A love appeal. To appeal to God's love from a place of relationship with God. God's love towards his people results in this loyal love and faithfulness, even when His people fail to be faithful.

To be beautiful - remain loyal and steadfast; steadfast in affection and allegiance; to remain firm in adherence to promises made.

But to what end will you TRULY be faithful?

Let's talk about it. **Numbers 22:21-39**

"Don't beat the donkey!"

"Strap yourself in and enjoy the ride!"

Today we meet a man by the name of Balaam – A lord of the people. A man who held rank among the people and was highly regarded and respected. He was hired by Balak, the king of Moab, to spoil things for the children of Israel.

Balak wanted Balaam to take the journey to where the Israelites had possessed and invaded the land – to curse them so that there would be no more. Balaam went against God's authority and took the journey anyway. It was a dangerous thing to make a decision and then ask God to bless what he did not sanction.

22 "But God was angry!"

Whenever we make decisions, always ensure that you get clearance and approval from God because it can cost you your life.

So now Balaam took a journey that angered God, and as a result, the Angel of the Lord was sent on a mission to take him out – enroute to the non-approved destination.

There were two servants and his trusted faithful steed donkey on the trip. And neither of the servants saw the Angel, only the donkey saw him. The donkey had a reputation of stubbornness and a strong sense of self-preservation. The donkey forgot about its own self-preservation and tried three evasive maneuvers to save his master.

"Don't beat the donkey!"

The first evasive maneuver : The Angel was standing in the middle of the road blocking the way. The donkey turned off the road onto the field, and Balaam beat the donkey. The donkey was being faithful and selfless, trying to stop his master's meeting with God's judgment. He was standing in love and being loyal and still got beat.

- Those who have gone out of their way to help others, to preserve their lives, to open doors of opportunity, are often the ones who are hurt when they find out they have been beaten down by the words and actions of other's, despite all the loyalty they have shown.

"Don't beat the donkey!"

The second evasive maneuver: The Angel blocked the narrow path so that the donkey could not move forward. And as a result, the donkey had no choice but to press close to the wall and accidentally crushed his master's foot. Once again, the donkey was beaten.

- There are people who takes on the full brunt of the weight of the situation. Meanwhile, the ones who only experience a minor crush are the ones who makes the most noise and beat down those who are literally fighting for their safety and survival.

"He's fighting for your survival!"

The third evasive maneuver: The Angel moved ahead to prevent the donkey from making movement in any direction. Then, the donkey did the only thing the donkey could do. He laid down, and again, he got beat.

When people who are wise enough to intervene and advise:
- Don't take another step.
- It's time to surrender.
- Danger! Danger! Danger! Danger!

Yet, for their words of wisdom, loyalty, and faithfulness, they got beat. Beat down by the people like Balaam. They want to do what they want to do, and they want to use you to get there. They are so focused on self that they miss the factor of danger.

"Don't beat the donkey!"

"Strap yourself in and enjoy the ride!"

- You beat me down once.
- You beat me down twice,
- You beat me down thrice.
- Now it's time to have a conversation.

[28] *"Then the Lord opened the donkey's mouth and it said to Balaam. What have I done to make you beat me these three times?"*

At some point in time, even from your heart of love and loyalty, you have to speak up and speak against what is being adversely done to you.

Balaam accused the donkey of making a fool of him and threatened to kill the donkey. Then the donkey had to remind Balaam of his loyalty to him as a donkey, with a running record, never has this type of behavior been involved. Balaam had to agree. When you do the right thing by the people who beat you down. Eventually, God himself will open their eyes to see:
- It was you carrying them all along.
- It was spiritual eyes that were guiding them.

- It was your heart of love and loyalty toward them that protected them all along.

When Balaam saw the Angel with his sword drawn, he fell face down.

"Don't beat the donkey!"

Angels are speaking for me in this season. The Angel told Balaam, if your donkey had not taken those evasive maneuvers, you would have been a dead man. And the donkey would have been spared.

There are some people who are wicked enough to verbally, mentally, emotionally, and even physically beat you down just like Balaam beat his donkey. But in this season, God is about to stop Balaam and that spirit of shame concerning you. Hallelujah!

"Don't beat the donkey!"

"Strap yourself in and enjoy the ride!"

Chapter 17

WHO IS VOUCHING FOR YOU?

What is Love?

Hegai (Heb) – Separation.

There is always a process or series of steps or actions to achieve levels of greatness. Greatness refers to the eminent qualities that distinguish you from everyone else in the room or world.

Greatness can be interpreted on many different levels and achieved in various spheres of life. For some people, their journey to greatness may have appeared to be seamless and effortless - but there is always a process that no one sees. The process is where the work is put in to get the results that everyone else sees.

People sit to enjoy a meal of succulent, tender ham, perfectly seasoned moist turkey, flavorful dirty rice, and the cheesiest, most delicious macaroni. But what they don't see on that plate is:

- ♦ The hours that were put into seasoning and basting the meats.
- ♦ The time of monitoring to ensure everything was cooked to perfection.

- The attention and love that was poured into the preparation.

People only see the end result.

People only taste the end result.

There is no second thought, no regard for what was done to get that meal plated. Today, we're going to look at the process of greatness for Queen Esther.

Esther 2:1-20

Esther's journey began when room was made for her because Queen Vashti failed to comply with what was required of her by the king. Esther was being brought in as a royal replacement.

Replacement (Heb) – Tankleef

Royal Replacement

Esther may have always been regal and fit to be magnificent, but now she was about to be royal.

The journey to greatness for Esther took her from being regal to royal. Because of her regal value and attributes, she was chosen among the other young virgins to be placed in the King Xerxes' Kingdom Haram, of which one would be named queen of the Kingdom. And even though she was regal, she could not make the cut alone on beauty and form. She needed someone on the inside to vouch for her.

Who's vouching for you?

Esther needed someone who was close to the king. She needed someone who knew the secrets of the selection process. She needed someone who could vouch for her above the other selected ladies.

The general process for everyone was to complete beauty preparations. And for this, the ladies chose whatever they wanted to beautify themselves with. But Esther's process was different. She was placed in custody of Hegai, the king's head Eunuch, and she came into favor and tender love with him.

The difference was, Esther didn't choose her own beauty regimen. She allowed the one who knew the King's likes, loves, and dislikes to set it up for her. Esther trusted his expertise, and Esther trusted his love.

When you are unwise in a certain area, you need to learn to trust the wisdom of the people who are experts in that area. When you lack the knowledge in a particular area, you need to connect with the people or organization that knows the matter through and through. In other words, you need them to stand in and vouch for you and to take what they know and make it easy for you.

Some people are know-it-alls. They:
- ♦ Refuse to accept knowledge greater than themselves.
- ♦ Refuse to listen to wisdom that outwits theirs.
- ♦ Hold on to pride, and they refuse to comply to help.

Greatness comes to those who are ready to trust the favor and tender love God sends into their lives.

Who's vouching for you?

Hegai was connected and close to the king. He knew exactly what the king liked and what the king was looking for. By trusting Hegai's decisions, she made her one night with the king far more distinguished from the crowd. The king had seen lot of breasts, thighs, lips, and eyes, but there was something different about Esther.

After one year of listening and obeying, the seed of greatness was achieved (365 days later). This speaks plainly – Greatness won't come in one night, but you have to trust the wisdom of the ones that God has placed in your life to lead you through the process to greatness.

Achieving greatness will become a challenge when you're:

- ♦ Jealous/envious of other people's achievements and of other people's favor.

Be OK:

- ♦ When your name isn't called.
- ♦ When others are favored over you.
- ♦ When you feel misplaced.

Why? Because after you are delivered and set free from jealousy and insecurities:

- ♦ Your name will be called.
- ♦ You will receive your due favour.
- ♦ You will then fit in.

Achieving greatness will be a challenge when you are stubborn and rebellious.

To be stubborn is showing unrelenting determination not to change one's attitude or position on something. Especially in spite of good arguments or reasoning.

Rebellious – is to show a desire to resist authority; to put up resistance.

Instead of being rebellious, be loyal, devoted, and steadfast. In other words, live the Hesed Love of God.

To be anything other than Hesed is to be rebellious.

Instead of being stubborn:
- ♦ Give in to the ways of God that can change your life.
- ♦ Allow self to die, stop allowing flesh to represent you (name brand apparel).
- ♦ Yield to the will of God completely and entirely.

Esther yielded to the knowledge, wisdom, and instruction of Hegai. And her wisdom to comply led to a night with the king that changed everything. Hegai, by doing all he did amidst Esther, was in fact vouching for her.

Vouch – To assert or confirm that someone is who they say they are.

Who is vouching for you?

Even if you are the "go-to" for so many people, you need a "go-to" too.

Even if you've been vouching for everyone else, eventually you will need someone to vouch for you.

When the right person vouches for you:
- ♦ Doors open with opportunities beyond your wildest dreams.
- ♦ You've been promoted from waiting to being waited on.
- ♦ You sit in seats of power and influence.

Who's vouching for you?

As you give allowance for the Hesed Love of God to manifest in your life, God will cause:
- ♦ People who are in a position to help you and to vouch for you.

- People who are in a position of influence to speak for you
- That which was hard for others will become easy for you.

God is sending the best of the best of the best to vouch for you! Come on and receive it! In Jesus's mighty name!

This is the season that Hegai will connect you with the king. One night with the king will change everything for the better and for the good in your life. Hallelujah!

Hesed – Love is Loyalty - Loyal love sprang up between Esther and Hegai, and it changed her whole world. Esther's unselfish act of love later changed the outcome for her nation.

Understand that when God leads you to greatness, it's always because he has a greater purpose.

Who's vouching for you?!

Chapter 18

Love – Your Round-Trip Ticket

What is Love?

Love is a powerful force; it causes people to yield their own wills and abandon all for the sake of the ones they love.

Love itself is defined as a profoundly strong affection for another person. But the Hesed Love of God outlasts all levels of love.

1. Ahab – Romantic Love (Heb)
2. Agape – Unconditional Love (Grk)
3. Philleo – Brotherly Love (friendship) (Grk)
4. Eros – Erotic Sexual Love/won't move past that moment
5. Pragra – Chooses to work with your partner
6. Storge – Parental Sacrificial Love
7. Ludus – Playful/Flirtatious Love
8. Mania – Obsessive/Jealous Love
9. Philaitia - Self Love/Sees Self Worth

There are 9 types of love, but there is a love that exists and supersedes them all.

Supersedes – Endures beyond normal capacity.

Persist – Continues to exist no matter the difficulty, opposition, or failure.

Faithful – Loyal will be on changing circumstances and steadfast in wavering moments.

Hesed - is a love that we crave beyond our knowledge. It is a love that we desire beyond our own understanding. It is a love that we desire beyond flesh. Hesed is an all-encompassing love.

Hesed is a "round-trip ticket". It won't just take you somewhere, it will bring you back. It will ensure that you securely arrive at your destination and will facilitate and accommodate your room for return.

Hesed Love won't get you stuck.

Stuck wondering:
- How do I move from here?
- How do I get to where I need to be?

Hesed love is supposed to:
- Inspire you
- Motivate you

Hesed is a love that is:
- Steadfast
- Enduring
- Rock-solid
- Faithful

Hesed is a love that is so enduring that it persists beyond any sin or betrayal to:
- Mend Brokenness
- To graciously extend forgiveness

Hesed – Love is Loyalty.

What is Love?

1 John 4:7-9

7 "Dear friends, let us love one another, for love comes from God. Everyone who loves has been born of God and knows God."

8 "Whoever does not love does not know God, because God is love. 9 This is how God showed his love among us: He sent his one and only Son into the world that we might live through him."

In other words, love is your identification card. It gives you confirmation of your connection to God, who is love.

Carry Your Love ID

1 John 3:1 - *"See what great love the Father has lavished on us, that we should be called children of God! And that is what we are! The reason the world does not know us is that it did not know him."*

Love is Your Access Code

Matthew 5:43-48

43 "You have heard that it was said, 'Love your neighbor[a] and hate your enemy.'

44 But I tell you, love your enemies and pray for those who persecute you,

45 that you may be children of your Father in heaven. He causes his sun to rise on the evil

⁴⁶*If you love those who love you, what reward will you get? Are not even the tax collectors doing that?*

⁴⁷*And if you greet only your own people, what are you doing more than others? Do not even pagans do that?*

⁴⁸*Be perfect, therefore, as your heavenly Father is perfect."*

Love is Your Boundary Breaker

1 John 3:18 - *"Dear children, let us not love with words or speech but with actions and in truth."*

Love is the movie ticket of your life!

Hesed Love is Loyalty:
- Wherever you go.
- Whatever you do.
- Whoever you meet.

Let love speak for you. Even when you're:
- Having a bad day.
- Down to your last dollar.
- Disappointed in some area.

Let love "Be What People See."

Hesed Love is Loyalty

Chapter 19

THE CAPACITY OF LOVE

What is love?

Hesed is the unique formulation of the love of God.

Love by itself can only be defined as a strong, passionate affection for another. But the difficulty with that is that passion can change on its Richter scale. The same way we see passion intensify is the same way it fizzles out and changes over time.

Hesed is the love that expresses God's faithfulness. Hesed is faithful, steadfast, rock solid, trustworthy, and enduring love.

Hesed Love is Loyalty

The Hesed love of God doesn't:
- Fizzle out
- Dintensify
- Lose power
- Gear down

The Hesed Love of God has the capacity or the ability to sustain its love position that is suited to every condition in your life. There is no limit when it comes to the love of God.

Exodus 34:6-7

vs. 6 "And he passed in front of Moses, proclaiming, "The Lord, the Lord, the compassionate and gracious God, slow to anger, abounding in love and faithfulness,

vs. 7 "Maintaining love to thousands, and forgiving wickedness, rebellion and sin. Yet he does not leave the guilty unpunished; he punishes the children and their children for the sin of the parents to the third and fourth generation."

Abounding in love means:
- ♦ To exist in large numbers or amounts.
- ♦ To have in large numbers or amounts

The capacity of God's love for "His People" is endless.

Endless Love

The same way God has proclaimed his endless, undying, unwavering, and unfaltering love for us, he has also placed a "Love Obligation" on "His People."

Declare: You are obligated to love me!

Obligated – to be compelled legally and morally to do something.

God himself placed this obligation on us.

Micah 6:8 - *"He has shown you, O mortal, what is good. And what does the Lord require of you? To act justly and to love mercy and to walk humbly[a] with your God."*

The message version of Micah 6:8 states:

vs 6 "But he's already made it plain how to live, what to do, what God is looking for in men and women."

vs 7 "it's quite simple: do what is fair and just to your neighbor, be compassionate and loyal in your love."

vs 8 "and don't take yourself too seriously but take God seriously."

In other words, the capacity of God's love lays obligation on us to:

1. To be fair, just, honest, and treat people right.
2. What you don't want done to you, don't do to others. (Cruelty/Harshness)
3. What you don't want said to you, don't say it to others. (Cussing/Harassing/Bullying)
4. When you fail to treat people right by what you do and say to them, God himself brings justice.

♦ He loves you but won't clear the guilt of what you've done. He will visit and send the bad ways and things you've done and said to others back to you and your children. Therefore, be careful how you treat people – full and final.

5. To be compassionate or to show kindness toward others.

♦ Being concerned about others genuinely, and not from the place of being intrusive or nosy. Be mature enough in your concern to pray well on the situation and not gossip about it.

1 Timothy 5:8 - "Anyone who does not provide for their relatives, and especially for their own household, has denied faith and is worse than an unbeliever."

This this is a disgrace in the sight of God.

6. To walk humbly with your God.

- To walk humbly is to be modest in your level of importance.
- Humility never wants to be seen or noticed.
- Humility is OK with putting everyone else ahead of oneself.
- Humbleness is necessary if you're going to walk with God because God doesn't walk with the arrogant or the proud.
- God resists the proud and gives grace to the humble.
- Don't put limits on how you love and who you love because to do so is not Hesed.

Chapter 20

Love Led Destiny

What is love?

Hesed Love is Loyalty

Love is defined as: a profoundly strong, tender, and passionate affection for another person.

But the Hesed Love of God is love on a premier level.

Hesed remains the same.

There are no variations or no fluctuations when it comes to the Hesed Love of God.

Hesed is a love that is steadfast, enduring, rock solid, faithful, and endures to eternity.

Hesed is a love that is so enduring that it persists beyond any sin or betrayal.

- ♦ To mend brokenness
- ♦ To graciously extend forgiveness

Today, we're going to see Hesed from a deeper place.

When someone has the Hesed, the love of God living and operating through them, they literally succumb to its power. No matter what is done or said to them.

Hesed Remains Respectful

In 1 Samuel 16, God sent the prophet Samuel to anoint David to be the next king of Israel. And from that moment, oil was poured forth, and David became a target and the aim of the attack. The enemy agent that was targeting him was King Saul.

When King Saul saw David's ability to lead, his favor with the people, his genuine purity of heart, and of course, he came into the knowledge that King David had been prequalified by God to replace him.

Divine Replacement

God thought about the people to make their own choice, and when that went awry, then God anointed the real deal for the takeover.

- David – The beloved of the Lord was the real deal.
- David ended up on the run. He literally tried to avoid confrontation and unnecessary battles with Saul, even though God had already promised to give him victory over his enemy.

You know you must really be a Kingdom threat when the king is trying to take you out. The enemy will pursue you when:

- Who you are innately infuses jealousy in them.
- They see what is in you is greater.
- You understand your place in destiny.

My Destiny is Great!

- ♦ David attempted to get out of the way to avoid confrontation.
- ♦ David was truly operating in the Hesed love of God.
- ♦ David had two opportunities to take Saul out by force, and in both instances, he walked away.

In the first instance, Saul was taking a bathroom break, and he was alone and vulnerable. But instead of taking Saul's life, David took a piece of Saul's robe to prove that he had Saul right where he wanted him. Yet, David did not hurt King Saul nor take his life.

David was in the company of warriors who saw the opportunity as one from God to eliminate the enemy and take the throne. But David's heart was steadfast in the Hesed love of God. Hesed wouldn't let David disrespect the anointing on Saul's life.

6 "He said to his men, the Lord forbid that I should do such a thing to my master the Lord's anointed of the Lord. "

The power of Hesed will cause you to respect those who disrespect you. People want to think it's OK to say crazy things to you or about you. However, your only response should be: Hesed Love is Loyalty. Your loyalty to the love of God will cause you to remain respectful.

So now… even after Saul's near encounter with death, he continued to pursue David, even though Saul admitted that David had not done anything against him. In Saul's continued pursuit, God gave David the tactical advantage over his enemy yet again.

This time God caused a deep sleep to come upon Saul and his entire army and David had another opportunity to kill Saul. Yet again, he spared Saul's life. The only thing David took was Saul's spear and a water jug as evidence that he was there and had his enemy in the palm of his hands and didn't squash him.

Hesed said, respect that anointing.

- David had every right to defend his life, but Hesed said, "No, don't touch God's anointed!"
- David had every right to retaliate, but Hesed said, "Let the Lord strike down the enemy."
- David had every right to deal with Saul the same way Saul dealt with him, but Hesed said, "Let the hand of God cause him to fall in battle."

2 Corinthians 10:4 - *"For the weapons of our warfare are not carnal but mighty through God to the pulling down of strongholds."*

As believers, we live by the word of the Lord, we do not resort to natural or carnal weapons to overcome those who oppose us. We pray and we bombard the heavens to silence our enemies.

As believers, we operate in the Hesed love of God that makes it seem like the enemy has the upper hand. When in fact, love gives you a greater advantage.

Just Love them Hesed

- God will release his judgment and wrath on your enemies.

Just Love them Hesed

- God will stop them from destroying your destiny.
- Take the level of the Hesed love of God in your life to the next level.

Hesed Love is Loyalty

- I love you enough to respect you.
- I love you enough to respect the authority on your life.
- I will not put my hands forth against the Lord's anointed.

Hesed

Chapter 21

WHAT A WONDERFUL WORLD IT WOULD BE!

What is love?

Hesed is the authentic love of God.

Love by definition is a profoundly strong, tender, and passionate affection for another person.

The Hesed Love of God is Love on a whole new level.

Whole New Level

Hesed is a love that is steadfast, enduring, rock solid, and faithful, and it endures to eternity.

Hesed is the kind of love that:
- Stands as a command over you and will never shift.
- Goes the distance with you no matter what you go through.
- Always forgives, no matter how deep or destructive the damage inflicted.

- Hesed will remain loyal to you and faithful, it won't cheat you nor cheat on you.

Hesed Love is how God loves us!

1. His commanded love never shifts.

2. His determined love goes the distance.

3. His compassionate love always forgives.

4. His loyal love stays faithful.

Wouldn't it be great if we all received this kind of love in our lives from people around us daily? What a Wonderful World it Would Be!

Love has the ability to draw us in. But most people base love on their level of emotional vulnerability, which often causes them to draw:

- Hope
- Motivation
- Peace
- Joy
- Aspiration
- Incentive

Some need these contacts with love in order to live.

God's Love – The Hesed Love of God has the power to sustain you through anything you go through. Hesed is the kind of love that shows up in action. It doesn't just say these 'three' words, "I love you!" But it actually gives life to these words because words are just words until they are enacted.

In Ruth 1:8, Naomi gave both of her daughters-in-law, Ruth and Orpah, the option to leave and return to their hometown. The word "kindness" she mentioned refers to the Hesed Love of God. She was advising them to rely on God's love because it was the only love that they could count on. After all, God's love never dies. God is life itself, and he cannot die. Therefore, all that he is will continue, even his love is forever.

Where forms of love have:
- Failed you
- Disappointed you
- Taken advantage of you
- Manipulated you
- Humiliated you
- Hurt you

The Hesed Love of God will never fail.

1 Corinthians 13:8 – *"Love never fails but where there are prophecies they will cease, where there are tongues, they will be stilled, where there is knowledge it will pass away."*

So, knowing this, why do people put so much emphasis on everything else other than the one unfailing force called love?

Hesed Love is Loyalty

If we all focused on connecting people to the love of God, the way Naomi and Ruth did…What a Wonderful World it Would Be!

Hosea 1:2 – *"When the Lord first spoke through Hosea, the Lord said to him go take for yourself a wife of prostitution and have children of her prostitution for the land commits great acts of prostitution by not following the Lord."*

Hosea, the prophet of God was commanded to marry and show love to Gomer – a prostitute. Gomer, being a prostitute from a line of prostitutes did what came naturally to her. She was unfaithful to her husband, and every time she walked away to be with other men, he retrieved her and literally bought her back.

Hesed love will be faithful even when other loves are unfaithful.

God expects us to be faithful to him as he is faithful to us. When we learned the depth of the Hesed love of God, faithfulness is birthed in us.

If everyone lived the Hesed Love of God and was faithful… What a Wonderful World it Would Be!

It's time for us to be faithful!

Faithful – (Heb) "Emunah

- Faithful
- Fidelity
- Steadfastness
- Firmness

To be faithful is to be steadfast and firm. Not easily swayed to go against what or who you love and what you hold.

What a Wonderful World This Would Be if:

- Husbands and wives are faithful to one another.
- Believers are faithful to their God assignments.
- Organizations are faithful to their employees.
- Governments are faithful to their citizens.

Judges 16:1,4-6

[1.] *"Now Samson went to Gaza and saw a harlot there, and went into her."*

[4.] *"Afterward it happened that he loved a woman in the Valley of Sorek, whose name was Delilah.*

⁵And the lords of the Philistines came up to her and said to her, "Entice him, and find out where his great strength lies, and by what means we may overpower him, that we may bind him to afflict him; and every one of us will give you eleven hundred pieces of silver."

⁶ So Delilah said to Samson, "Please tell me where your great strength lies, and with what you may be bound to afflict you."

By the looks of things, Samson was a man driven by the appetite of his flesh. Sounds like someone was:

- Looking for love in all the wrong places.
- Looking for love in too many faces.

Samson did not know faithfulness, but he desired faithfulness. But know this…

Galatians 6:7 - *"Be not deceived; God is not mocked: for whatsoever a man soweth that shall he also reap."*

Therefore - memo to Sampson. If you want faithfulness and loyalty – you must sow faithfulness and loyalty. If you want love, you must sow love. If up until now you have genuinely sown good and it's not being returned or reciprocated, just know this:

- The shift is on
- The move is on.
- The transfer is on.
- The conveyance is on.
- The switch is on.
- God is getting ready to switch out the old with the new!
- God is getting ready to switch out the bad with the good!
- God is getting ready to switch out the fake love for the real deal!

What a Wonderful World it Would Be!

Now, pertaining to Samson, he ended up resting his head in the lap of a woman who did not know how to be loyal to anyone other than herself…Hesed Love is Loyalty

Delilah wanted Samson to divulge his secrets so that she could hit the big time/the lottery/jackpot from the five lords.

It hurts when you have shown loyalty to the disloyal. It hurts when the loyalty you expected never shows up. And in the eventuality of things for Samson, that disloyal relationship cost him his life.

Today, I challenge you to disconnect from disloyal and disruptive relationships in Jesus' name.

If everyone in our lives lived the Hesed as we lived the Hesed… What a Wonderful World it Would Be!

Chapter 22

FINISH STRONG!

What is love?

Hesed is marked by God's authentic extension of himself as love.

Love by definition: A profoundly strong, tender, and compassionate affection for another person.

However, the Hesed Love of God extends more:
- More faithfulness
- More steadfastness
- More endurance
- More loyalty

There are no limits or limitations to the operation of the love of God – Hesed.

Hesed:
- Stands as a command over your life, and it will never shift.
- Walks the distance with you, no matter what you go through.

- ♦ Always forgives and remains loyal to you, won't beguile or cheat on you.

Just as God commanded this love toward us, God commands us to love.

1 John 4:8 - *"Anyone who does not love, does not know God because God is love."*

In order to love others, you must first know God.

John 13:34-35 -

vs 34. "A new commandment I give to you, that you love one another; as I have loved you, that you also love one another.

vs. 35. "By this all will know that you are My disciples, if you have love for one another."

God commands us to love so that we can be the right representation of him in the Earth.

Nehemiah's heart was indeed showing the very nature of God – Hesed.

Nehemiah was living and working in a foreign land. But his heart's position never shifted concerning wanting to help his country and his people. Nehemiah's stance was that of a patriot. The Hesed Love of God is Patriotic.

Patriot is defined as: A person who vigorously supports their country and is prepared to defend it against enemies or detractors.

Detractor: A person who disparages someone or something.

Disparage: regard or represent as being of little worth.

Hesed – Love is Loyalty – Love is Patriotic

Hesed is the kind of love that will defend you the way Nehemiah defended his God assignment.

Nehemiah 4:17 - *"Those who built on the wall, and those who carried burdens, loaded themselves so that with one hand they worked at construction, and with the other held a weapon."*

When the detractors showed up to talk "smack," he gave them no attention. Why? He was loyal. His love for God was Hesed.

People who operate in the Hesed love of God are loyal. They are defenders of those they love. They won't stand around and let:

- Your name be unduly scandalized.
- Your character assassinated by enemies.
- Your life being brought under wicked scrutiny.

People who love you – Hesed – are loyal to you.

Let me test your loyalty:

1. Do you believe in me and my natural God-given abilities?

2. Do you allow others to talk about me or to bring me down and say nothing?

3. Do you act loyal, but at the first sign of upheaval, you throw me under the bus using all you know about me against me?

4. Do you stand around with me in hard times or only when it's time to shine?

Hesed Love is Loyalty – Love is Patriotic - Hesed Operated in Nehemiah.

Nehemiah wanted to see his nation's walls restored and his people protected.

Hesed desires to see you protected. In other words, Hesed wants what's best for you and is not selfish to covet all for itself.

Nehemiah had a high official position in serving the Persian king. He didn't have to worry about his nation or his nation's walls. But love wouldn't let him!

There were many times I'm sure you wanted to:

- Do your own thing.
- Go your own way.
- Say what you like.
- Do what you like.

But Hesed's love wouldn't let you!

Nehemiah 6:3 - *"So, I sent messengers to them, saying, "I am doing a great work, so that I cannot come down. Why should the work cease while I leave it and go down to you?"*

Nehemiah was loyal and patriotic; he refused to allow his detractors to distract him. Loyalty will cause you to set your priorities in order. Loyalty will cause you to maintain focus on what's important.

Nehemiah was driven by love – Hesed Love is Loyalty. He not only completed his assignment, but he also finished Strong!

In this season, in order to finish strong, you must:

1. Put distance between you and those who want to separate you from what God has called you to do!

2. Disregard and pay little attention to those who attempt to devalue and belittle you.

In other words,

- Know your assignment.
- Know you're assignor.
- Know your value.

When God entrusts you, remember you already carry the anointing to finish strong.

Hesed Love is Loyalty – Love is Patriotic

Chapter 23

Love Intervenes

What is love?

Hesed is the kind of love that flows from the heart of God. It is a steadfast love that remains constant no matter what evil is done against it.

Hesed is rock-solid and has the capacity to endure. It never gives up on you.

Hesed is the ultimate meaning of going the distance.

Hesed far exceeds any type of superficial vows, passion, fleeting affection, or wavering desire.

Hesed goes deep and can be translated as:

- ♦ Mercy: compassion or forgiveness shown towards someone who is within one's power to punish or harm.

Remember David and Saul? David had every earthly and natural right to kill Saul for attempting to kill him by putting out a 'hit' on his life. But David's response was Hesed.

1 Samual 26:9 - *"And David said to Abishai, Destroy him not: for who can stretch forth his hand against the LORD's anointed, and be guiltless?*

Hesed goes deep and can be translated as:

Goodness – The quality of being morally good or virtuous. (Having high moral standards.)

Boaz: Boaz went to the people in power to rescue Naomi and her right of inheritance. He did that which was an act of goodness. Understand, he was already wealthy, and he didn't need anything. He was not obligated to purchase the land and the right of inheritance. Yet, he acted in goodness (Hesed), and God caused no one else to be interested in that land so that Boaz could be awarded with it.

Understand that Hesed love cannot see you in a bad situation and leave you there. Hesed Love is Loyalty and will always intervene.

Ruth 4:9-10

⁹ "Then Boaz announced to the elders and all the people, "Today you are witnesses that I have bought from Naomi all the property of Elimelek, Kilion, and Mahlon."

¹⁰ "I have also acquired Ruth the Moabite, Mahlon's widow, as my wife, in order to maintain the name of the dead with his property, so that his name will not disappear from among his family or from his hometown. Today you are witnesses!"

Boaz intervened and preserved the family name… Hesed Love is Loyalty

Love Will Always Intervene

Love wants to:
- ♦ See you improve.
- ♦ Stand with you in difficult times.

- See your life meet destiny.

That's why goodness and mercy follow us all the days of our lives (Psalm 23) because of the power of God's love. In other words, God says my love won't let you go through what you're going through alone.

Hesed goes deep and can be translated as:
- Faithful: Remaining steadfast and true to the original.
- Hesed is the kind of love that keeps its word.
- People often say they love you, but their actions prove they don't know God. Because to know God is to love the way he loves.
- Hesed is faithful; it won't switch up on you. God is faithful.

Have you ever considered, "What if God was one of us?" Listen to me - we would be in the deepest trouble. Because people are fickle and double-minded. One minute they are for you, and the next minute they are listening to satan's radio station in their mind and coming up against you.

So, from now on, when people say they love you, ask them what radio station frequency is your love tuned to? Is it a freshly satanic love that changes your mind, switches your heart, and makes you take back the blessing that you said,

"God said to give me."

OR

Your Hesed, no matter what changes your love will remain steadfast and faithful.

Psalm 15:1 - *"Lord, who may dwell in your sacred tent? Who may live on your holy mountain?*

God is about to refuse some people because of how they treated you. Where they thought they were in God, they're about to find out they don't have a foot to stand on.

Hesed Love – Keeps your word, full and final.

Hesed goes deep and can be translated as loyal:

Loyal: giving or showing firm constant support or allegiance to a person or institution.

- True loyalty cannot be switched on and off like a light bulb. It's always constant.
- True loyalty cannot be permeated by external forces. It's always holding on to the original vow.
- True loyalty cannot be bought with money, bribes, or papers. It's always standing in integrity.

God is Hesed – Love is Loyalty.

God wants us to become Hesed. God wants us to shine Hesed everywhere we go! Hesed!

When you are truly connected to God, Hesed operates in you:

- Loyalty is easy.
- Faithfulness is easy.
- Goodness is easy.
- Mercy is easy.

God is love, and he can identify with the people who truly know his love. It's a downright dirty shame to see people who say they have lived decades for God, and they are still:

- Causing Confusion in the church.
- Undermining leadership in the church.
- Seeking to infiltrate and bring unnecessary battles.

Hesed operates in honesty, integrity, and openness.

- Hesed is transparent.
- God is Hesed.
- God is transparent.

Before he brings impending judgment, he tells you. Before he blesses you, he tells you to expect it's on the way.

Isaiah 42:9 - *"See, the former things have taken place, and new things I declare; before they spring into being, I announce them to you."*

- Hesed love will never lead you to the dark.
- Hesed love will never leave you in the dark.

HESED!

Chapter 24

Even to our Enemies

What is love?

Jonah – (Heb) – Dove

Doves are symbols of:
- Peace
- Messengers
- Love
- Ninevah – (Heb) – Handsome; agreeable.
- Tarshish – (Heb) – Breaking; subjection; contemplation; examination.
- Amitti – (Heb) – Truth

Jonah was a prophet of God. A prophet who had been given the assignment of proclaiming the judgment of God to Ninevah (they were good-looking and agreeable people).

The inhabitants of Ninevah had been practicing wickedness, and the broaden extent of the wickedness had reached the heavens. Therefore, God had to intervene.

Always remember that when God wants to intervene in the earth, he raises up and uses a prophet. In other words, God gives the prophet the legal license to speak from the heart of God. One might think it's such an honor to be used by God, but Jonah was a runner.

Jonah couldn't wait to hit the road and take a journey into the furthest region opposite the place of his assignment. But what Jonah failed to understand was, there is no place you can hide or run to escape the presence of the Lord.

By refusing to obey God, Jonah fell out of synchronization and syncopation with God. To be synchronized is to operate at the same time, rate, and place. To be syncopated is to be connected and moving in the same rhythmic motion. Jonah and his outright blatant decision to disobey God found himself:

- In the wrong place
- At the wrong time

And as a result of being in the wrong place at the wrong time, Jonah caused trouble. The brew of a violent storm developed on the sea, and the ship was about to break up. Being in the wrong place at the wrong time can cost you!

Lord, Keep Me Synchronized and Syncopated to your Heartbeat

In the eventuality of things, it was discovered that by Jonah being on board of the ship to Tarshish, he was the root of the problem.

In order to alleviate any problem in your life, you must deal with the root by pulling it out. To just pull off the visible protrusions is not going to stop the situation from re-emerging. Why? Because when the roots remain, so does the issue.

A lot of people mask the issues in their lives by removing the problematic areas that are visible. But the problem or situation will always recur because the root has never been dealt with.

For example: people who come from abject poverty usually become hoarders who are greedy with avarice and love to get money.

For example: some people have emotional issues. They pull off the top part of the issue by faking their way through relational situations instead of dealing with the root cause of the issues, such as:

- Hatred
- Bitterness
- Envy
- Covetous
- Unforgiveness
- Jealousy
- Animosity
- Anger

When you come to a place and you want to mature in the things of God, you have to pull out the root.

Pull Out the Root

Jonah was the root of the problematic storm; therefore, he had to be pulled out and literally thrown overboard. Listen, when you're in the wrong place – where God didn't send you – wrong time - when God didn't place you there, you will create trouble for the innocent.

Do what God told you. Go where God sent you.

Amazingly enough, the Bible says that when the men found Jonah, he was sleeping. Isn't it amazing that those who cause the trouble gets the pleasure of sweet sleep, while you're dealing with the full extent of the issue? Jonah slept through the storm, even though the damage he caused was against the innocent.

Jonah 1:15 - *"So they picked up Jonah, I threw him into the sea, and the sea stopped raging."*

Memo to the believers

When you throw "Jonah" overboard, the trouble you've been dealing with for years will cease to exist.

Jonah may have been en route to contemplation – Tarshish – but God gave him a place of incubation, the belly of the whale.

Jonah had to sit for three days. Biblical numerology 3 represents:

- Harmony
- Completeness
- God's presence

God gave Jonah three days of his presence to bring him into complete harmony.

When you find that people are moving and rebelling against you, eventually they will be placed and positioned for a "sit down". Jonah had been sat down by God.

The reality of the situation was, Jonah didn't want to go and warn the people because he viewed them as his enemies. He wanted God to just take them out. Jonah wanted God to execute his executive order without warning because he knew if the people (his enemies) repented, God would forgive them.

Hesed Love is Loyalty

Guess what? The love of God – Hesed operates without exception, even for your enemies, and Jonah was right.

Jonah 3:10 – *"When God saw what they did and how they turned from their evil ways, he relented and did not bring on them the destruction he had threatened."*

The people repented, and God's faithful compassion and mercy intervened…Hesed.

God forgave them.

There was an apparent issue in the heart of Jonah. Jonah had an issue with seeing his enemy's escape:

- Utter devastation
- Terrible torture
- Deliberate disaster

He wanted to see them be punished severely as his enemies, but never forget the power of God's love. Hesed Love is Loyalty even to our enemies.

Matthew 5:43-48

[43]. *"You have heard that it was said, 'Love your neighbor[a] and hate your enemy."*

[44]. *"But I tell you, love your enemies and pray for those who persecute you,"*

[45]. *"that you may be children of your Father in heaven. He causes his sun to rise on the evil and the good and sends rain on the righteous and the unrighteous. "*

⁴⁶. *"If you love those who love you, what reward will you get? Are not even the tax collectors doing that?"*

⁴⁷. And if you greet only your own people, what are you doing more than others? Do not even pagans do that?"

⁴⁸. "Be perfect, therefore, as your heavenly Father is perfect."

It's time for us to perfect the way we love each other.

Hesed Love is Loyalty, even to our enemies.

Chapter 25

Divine Kindness

What is love?

Hesed is the Ultimate Form of Love…

Hesed is the Love of God…

Hesed Love is Loyalty…

Hesed is deeper than superficial emotion. Hesed is more vast than fleeting affection. Hesed is more pure than pulsating passion. Hesed is the kind of love that is:

- Steadfast
- Faithful
- Merciful
- Committed
- Gracious
- Rock solid
- Compassionate
- Generous
- Reliable
- Forgiving

Today, we're talking about what it means to allow the love of God – Hesed to be the kindness in us and through us.

Kindness: Showing friendly gestures with a generous intent and a considerate nature.

Kindness should be a part of everyone's day-to-day life. Being kind to others won't take anything away from who you are. So why is it that so many people have an issue with being kind?

Proverbs 11:17 - *"A man who was kind benefits himself, but a cruel mind hurts himself."*

There are benefits or advantages to be gained when you show kindness.

Hesed Love is Loyalty & Kindness

Showing kindness to others often puts prideful people in an odd position. Mainly because they are usually too conceited or arrogant to bother being kind. It takes a humble heart to render kindness.

1 John 3:18 - *"My little children, let us not love in word or in tongue, but in deed and in truth."*

"In Deed" refers to the doings of kindness. One act of kindness shows people, not only that you care but that love does exist. Love is the motivating factor in the heart that motivates kindness in us. That's why it's incredibly difficult for someone who does not know love to be genuinely kind. Not just showing kindness to those you can benefit from, but from those who could never repay you.

Proverbs 19:17 - *"Whoever is generous to the poor lends to the Lord and he will repay him for his deed."*

God blesses you when you're kind toward the poor, and he repays you for your kindness. Kindness is a matter of the heart, conditioned by the mind. You have to have a generous mindset in order for kindness to work in and through you. Kindness demands that you place no limits on your level of kindness and do so without discrimination. To be kind is to love and express love – Hesed.

1 Corinthians 13:4 - *"Love is patient, it is kind, love does not envy or both and it is not arrogant."*

When you show kindness, help someone, or give to someone, you should never boast arrogantly about it. As a believer, there must be evidence of Hesed – Love of God in your life. Kindness is evidence.

1 John 3:17 - *"But if anyone has the world's goods and sees his brother in need yet closes his heart against him how does God's love abide in him?"*

In other words, when God allows you to be blessed with material goods, he expects you to be generous and kind, not stingy or mean.

Some people only give when they want others to see them.
- ♦ That's not genuine kindness.

Some people only give to others what they don't want.
- ♦ That's not genuine kindness.

Some people only give to those who can give back to them.
- ♦ That's not genuine kindness.

Romans 15:2 - *"Let each of us please his neighbor for it is good to build him up."*

Another way to show kindness is to build people up and bless their lives in every area.
- ♦ A kind word.
- ♦ A hug.

- ♦ A smile.

It all goes a long way, and it pleases God when we treat others with kindness. And this is a part of God, and it's what he desires from us.

Micah 6:8 - *"What does the Lord require of you, to do justly, love mercy (kindness), and to walk humbly before God."*

Never miss your chance to love on others or show kindness because you may never get another opportunity. Remember, God would never ask us to do what he would not be willing to do as well. God shows us plainly; He is founded in kindness.

Isaiah 54:10 -

"For the mountains shall depart

And the hills be removed,

But my kindness shall not depart from you,

Nor shall My covenant of peace be removed,"

Says the Lord, who has mercy on you."

Follow the heart of Father God and be founded in kindness.

1 Peter 3:8-9 -

vs.8. *"Finally, all of you be of one mind, having compassion for one another; love as brothers, be tenderhearted, be [a]courteous;"*

vs. 9. *"Not returning evil for evil or reviling for reviling, but on the contrary blessing, knowing that you were called to this, that you may inherit a blessing."*

Kindness rules. It overrides what you want to do and what you think you should do. Love with the *love* of kindness upon your lips. God will be pleased with you. Hesed.

Chapter 26

WHAT YOU WON'T DO – DO FOR LOVE

You've tried everything – but you won't give up.

What is love?

Everybody, no matter their situation or position in life desires love; to love and to be loved. The very desire for love and to be loved comes from the heart of the master architect…The Most High God Yahweh.

God was so filled with love because it was the essence of his being; he needed someone to express his love to. And thus, his ingenious plan to create you and me. For God so loved everyone in the world that he gave a part of his love to be sacrificed. Doing so, he allowed everyone he created to have the opportunity to live eternally and to experience his love forever.

- ♦ God's love for you is a forever love.
- ♦ God's love knows no ending.
- ♦ God loves his infinite in nature.

Just as vehement is God's desire to have a love relationship with all his children. There's nothing that God won't do for those who love him genuinely – genuinely hearing and obeying God's commandments.

Love is an action word!

Love is a command!

And by command we love!

What you won't do – Do for Love

Love does take some doing. Yet, it was never God's intention for you to put yourself in a place of disadvantage because you want the advantage of someone loving you.

Judges 16:18-20 -

18. "And when Delilah saw that he had told her all his heart, she sent and called for the lords of the Philistines, saying, Come up this once, for he hath shewed me all his heart. Then the lords of the Philistines came up unto her, and brought money in their hand."

19. "And she made him sleep upon her knees; and she called for a man, and she caused him to shave off the seven locks of his head; and she began to afflict him, and his strength went from him."

20. "And she said, The Philistines be upon thee, Samson. And he awoke out of his sleep, and said, I will go out as at other times before, and shake myself. And he wist not that the Lord was departed from him."

Samson put himself in a state of disadvantage because he wanted the advantage of love, but it didn't work.

Samson put his heart in the hands of a:
- ♦ Manipulator: She handled him unscrupulously.

- Betrayer: She exposed him and delivered him to his enemy.
- Humiliator: She made fun of him and brought him shame and loss of dignity.

Know this! The love God assigns you will never manipulate, humiliate, or be arbitrary to you.

You can't love so badly that you move blindly. You need to move with wisdom, especially when it comes to matters of the heart and loving people on any level.

Proverbs 4:23 - *"Above all else, guard your heart for it determines the course of your life."*

Love would never allow you to be overtaken or take a loss by underhanded plans. Everyone is not going to come clean about who they are and what they intend to do regarding you. That's why you must love God more than anyone or anything. An enriched love relationship with God will keep you centered and focused so that you will never be:

- Mishandled: where you're dealt with wrongly and roughly.
- Mismanage: to treat someone badly.

People with evil intentions will always mishandle and mismanage others intentionally. But they won't do it until they have you exactly where they want you.

Today, I break loose from being mishandled and mismanaged.

In Genesis 30, Jacob was mishandled and mismanaged by his family and his uncle Laban. Yes, I know you want to be loved but let God do it because your flesh will mess you up every time.

Instead, keep your spiritual eyes open and allow God to move in your intimate, personal, and familial relationships.

Love has a built-in characteristic, and when applied properly, it will build you up and not tear you down. It will cause you to build up others and not tear them down.

What you won't do – Do for Love

Love is a vital necessity for the existence of life. But it's not intended for you to allow someone else's darkness to overtake you and smother the light that God has called you to be. Never allow your pursuit of love and all that it encompasses to put up with:

- Toxic Situations
- Demonic Drama
- Satanic Interference

All of which brings the gloom and doom of depression.

- Love should enlighten you, not depress you.
- Love should excite you, not suppress you.
- Love should come with freedom, not oppress you.

The love of God Hesed is:

- Loyal and Faithful
- Steadfast and Rock-Solid
- Generous and Compassionate
- Covenant and Committed
- Kind and Dependable

If the love that you're experiencing is not encompassing those traits, you need to pray. This way God can intervene and bring you into the fullness of what love needs to be for you.

Deuteronomy 4:9 - *"Only be on your guard and diligently water yourselves, so that you do not forget the things your eyes have seen and so they do not slip from your heart as long as you live. Teach them to your children and grandchildren."*

When you know better, yeah, you do better. Pass along the wisdom you've acquired.

Lord, bring love into my life on all levels that is loyal, genuine, committed, faithful, kind, gentle, generous, and dependable. Amen!

When that kind of love manifests in your life, then your heart will be in the right position to love and to be loved. What you won't do – Do for Love

Chapter 27

ON DEMAND

What is love?

We have come to understand that the implementation of modern technology makes the use of gadgets more accommodating. The days of old are gone when we had to:

- Wait to eat because you had to reheat everything on the stove and in the pot.

Now we have a microwave.

- Wait to get off one call to receive another.

Now we have call waiting.

- Get up and walk to the television to change the channel.

Now we have remote controls and plug-and-play systems.

The system upgrades of the world have pushed past the old, and we must do the same.

On Demand

Here we witness another powerful Kingdom principal parable. A widow who found herself in a place of desperation. She was in a place of despair, her rights were being violated, and she needed the law to stand up and protect her. She needed the law to rise up and speak in her favor. Nevertheless, she persisted daily in going after what she wanted. To make matters worse, her case was before:

- An atheist
- A shrewd, cruel man

Desperation will birth persistence in your life. When desperation meets a stubborn situation, it has to give way. Her desperation and persistence got the judge's attention.

Can you imagine him seeing her over and over and over on the same matter? He must have been thinking, "YOU AGAIN?!"

It's time to get desperate because desperation shifts atmospheres.

- Hannah was desperate, and God gave her a baby from a barren womb.
- The woman with the issue of blood was desperate when she was healed of her issue immediately.
- Blind Bartimaeus was so desperate that he started a ruckus that ended with him receiving his sight.

On Demand

Desperation will get the hand of God to move for you. The widow pushed through the same way we are to push through.

We are now in a season that God is saying. "Pray it Forward"

Pray it Forward

The widow was persistent, so the judge decided to give her what she was requesting from the law.

I declare over you! There are some affluent people getting ready to make some decisions about you, and in your favor. The Lord's gavel has concluded the matter in your favor.

Repeat after me…**The order has been handed down in my favor!**

The same way the widow got what she wanted and walked away victorious; God wants the same for you. God wants you in a place in the Kingdom of God where, when you ask or petition for anything, you will receive it. Now, flow with me into this revelation.

On Demand

We often assimilate "On Demand" while watching movies. When a movie is scheduled at a particular time, you will be given preferential access to watch that movie whenever you so choose; all you have to do is click.

On Demand

I know that gets some people excited, but here's the plugin. In order to access "On Demand," you have to upgrade from being basic. Yes, you have to upgrade from:

- Doing what the worldly others are doing.
- Responding to situations in a worldly and carnal way.
- Seeing yourself as common, ordinary, or irrelevant.

Upgrade to the *Silver Package* and click "On demand". Silver is the symbol for purification. The silver package is where your life has been purged from the dross. Your silver package qualifies you for the next level.

On Demand

On the next level, you can upgrade to the *Gold Package*. In other words, you will upgrade to a place where:

- Your faith is no longer easily shaken.
- Your position in the Kingdom is indestructible. No matter what comes at you, you come out smelling like a rose and shining bright as a diamond.
- You literally dwell in a divine sphere where you are connected to heaven and in your relationship with God.

On Demand

When you upgrade to your "*Gold Package*":

- You no longer have to wait for the regularly scheduled program.
- You need to know. Get it now!

It gets even better. You can upgrade to the *Platinum Level*. In other words, you level up to a strength that you never had before. A strength:

- To bypass temptation.
- To stand up in moral uprightness.
- To display the love of God to a hateful world.
- The press beyond the point that has kept your life at a standstill.
- To endure hardness as good soldiers.
- To allow people to take advantage of you, so God can bring you out into a wealthy place.

Are you ready for the upgrade?
- **Silver**
- **Gold**
- **Platinum.**

There is no "On Demand" access on the basic package level. It's time to,

- Be driven by desperation.
- Be pushed into persistence.
- Break away from waiting for the regular scheduled program.
- Receive your blessings (whatever it may be for you).

And get your blessings ON DEMAND!

Silver! Gold! Platinum!

It's time to upgrade!

Hallelujah!

Scan QR Code or visit
apostlerochellegrahamministries.org
to purchase books.

www.ingramcontent.com/pod-product-compliance
Lightning Source LLC
Chambersburg PA
CBHW070550170426
43201CB00012B/1796